It Really Happened Here!

BY
ETHELYN PEARSON

IT REALLY HAPPENED HERE!

Author - Ethelyn Pearson
Publisher - McCleery & Sons Publishing

International Standard Book Number: 0-9700624-5-1
Printed in the United States of America.

ACKNOWLEDGMENTS

Dozens of cooperative resources made the gathering of information found in this book possible. It is with trepidation that I make this list, fearful of leaving out some valuable contributing source. Stories came via old books, ledgers, newspapers, and micro film found in the archives of The Hewitt Historical Society Museum, Wadena County Historical Museum, East Otter Tail County Museum in Perham, Todd County Historical Museum in Long Prairie, Stevens County Historical Museum in Morris, Clay County Historical Society, and the Bertha Historical Society Museum. Newspapers who proved to be useful were Staples World, Wadena Pioneer Journal, Long Prairie Leader, Independent Herald in Clarissa, The Fargo Forum, The Morris Tribune, Fergus Falls Daily, and Brainerd Dispatch. Libraries used were The Wadena City Library, The Moorhead State University Library, Morris City Library, City Library in Park Rapids, and the Sam Brown Historical Center in Brown's Valley, South Dakota. Special thanks to Pastor Vern Burgeson, Wadena, who allowed me to make use of his extensive library, to Robert Zosel for opening files (it took him long hours to assemble), to Administrator Michael Gibson of Shady Lane Nursing Home in Wadena who realized the value of the true stories his residents had to tell and encouraged my taking time during a workday to write them down.

Sincere gratitude and appreciation to a fine publisher, Hap McCleery, and my editor, Steve Tweed, the most skilled and patient of editors anywhere who whipped my stories into a book I can be proud of. Long stemmed red roses to Dr. S. Fred Everett, fine doctor and valued friend, who was instrumental in getting "writer" and "publisher" together. Lastly my thanks to Wadena and the community for being a great place to raise a family, live and become a senior citizen.

Ethelyn Pearson

INTRODUCTION

Ethelyn Pearson strode into our office one bright spring day and presented McCleery and Sons Publishing a chance to publish some of the region's rich history. Our lives have never been the same since those first editorial meetings.

We are energized and inspired by this wonderful Minnesotan, who gets things done a lot faster than people in the ninth decade are supposed to. We have met Ethelyn; but the added bonus is that we have also met her wild and brave characters, drawn from true life stories in Minnesota and the Dakotas. She serves up her memories and rural legends in humorous prose, alive with wit and country bred irony. A columnist and feature writer for years, Ethelyn Pearson is beloved by her community and her family. Now that we know her, she is truly admired at McCleery and Sons Publishing.

Our upper Midwest people are lucky to have chroniclers like Ethelyn, who keep stories of the old days alive and interesting. We may not live in the most frequently covered region by media on the national scene, but that makes our history all the more fascinating. Sometimes, it's just plain amazing that "It Really Happened Here."

Steve Tweed
Editorial Director
McCleery and Sons Publishing

DEDICATION

In loving memory of a great mom who treasured every word I wrote and saved them all, and of a husband, Milton Pearson, who shared an interest in history with me and listened to hundreds of my stories that never saw print.

Also in appreciation of my children, Larry (and Pat) Pearson, Arlen (and Norma) Pearson, and Linda (and Don, deceased) Bokinskie, who upon occasion let me write about them. I am proud to claim eight grandchildren and six little great-great's.

TABLE OF CONTENTS

Two-Gun Bill, the bank robber and booze runner!

When Two Gun Bill Henderson boasted "When I clean 'em, they're cleaned!", he meant it. The First State Bank of Hewitt could attest to it. At about 9:30 on May 2, 1931, Hiliary Henderson, also known as "Two Gun Bill", stepped inside the Hewitt bank flourishing a gun. He shattered the quiet, along with the nerves of cashier Ed Thompson and assistant Florence Wendorf, by ordering "Face down on the floor. This is a holdup!" Two unfortunate customers who came by soon joined those already on the floor. As Thompson, who could only be described as a portly gent at best, dropped to the floor, he pressed a button that alerted the Hewitt hardware store, two doors down. Proprietor Alex Moodie was caught unprepared,

with only a .22 caliber rifle on hand.

By the time suitable arms were found and someone to man them, Henderson and his partner and wheel-man, Clarence W. Campbell, had disappeared down one of the four roads that led out of Hewitt. Since there was more dust in the air toward the west, Moodie went thataway, armed only with his fists and a big mouth, qualities he found quelled most folks.

The bandits had been watching the bank for several days. Once Two Gun Bill had made the bust, he stood guard while Campbell took his time cleaning the bank out of a sum of $2,400.00. Locking bankers and customers in the vault, they high tailed it out of town toward

Two Gun Bill drove down this Hewitt street unnoticed on the way to the Watkins farm.

Wrightstown, entrance to "the swamp." Soon authorities in several counties were alerted. Kenneth Adams, deputy sheriff and son of Sheriff S.L. Adams came from Long Prairie, county seat of Todd County. Sheriff John Bengston, Chief of Police R.C. Kassube and Patrolman Abe Lee responded from Wadena. Eventually, bloodhounds from Redwood Falls were ordered in. A hoard of men from Hewitt, Wadena, Bertha and Long Prairie made up a respectable-sized posse.

Under cover of darkness that very evening, the quarry turned up their nose at their pursuers by sneaking up to the Watkins house, bordering the swamp, for something to eat. It can be assumed that Two Gun Bill and Campbell were mighty pleased with themselves as snug in their lair they heard frustrated lawmen shouting, running every whichway, lights crisscrossing fields and pastures. After several days of this, they successfully slipped away.

In retrospect, lawmen from every quarter made botch after botch. For instance: the alarm went into Alex Moodie's hardware store only to find him unprepared. Bloodhounds were called in too late, after the terrain was a maze of tracks. Sheriff Adams spent valuable time putting surveillance on a cold hideout. Bengston shot wildly in frustration into thin air in the direction the tracks led from the robbers' empty car. The bandits slipped the net

not once, but twice! After three days, the chase was called off and everyone returned home. Licked.

On October 13, 1931, Two Gun Bill and Campbell were apprehended in Wichita, Kansas, for the robbery of a bank at Haysville. They were arrested in a rooming house shortly after stealing $178. The pair also admitted to robberies in Judson and Meridan, as well as several in Iowa, to total an amount nearing $75,000. They ended up in the Kansas state penitentiary serving sentences which were from ten to fifty years each. Claude, Fay and Valto Watkins were arraigned, found guilty for harboring criminals, and sentenced to terms ranging from one to three years in Stillwater.

In 1925, Henderson was a rum runner in Waseca. It was in that year that his car, loaded with fifteen gallons of booze, was struck by a switch engine. In an ugly mood, Henderson had the audacity to demand a settlement from the railroad. He was arrested and brought into district court.

Henderson's character make-up presented a study in contradictions. Termed by officials to be one of the hardest, most daring of criminals, when Two Gun Bill heard himself being sentenced in 1925 to pay a fine of $300 and ninety days in jail, with sentence suspended on payment of the fine, he fainted dead away!

Modesty still meant something when this woman's pants fell down!

You could see a piece down the road both north and south where Louie and Lidy Gossell lived. They could hear the sound of metal buggy wheels on the dirt road before they could see the rig. Today there was something wrong. The buggy, a fancy one, pulled into sight by a fine animal that was definitely in trouble. It took short, choppy strides. Threw its head this way and that. Acted like it wanted to lay down right in harness.

The man driving edged it along until they came to the Gossell's driveway and then turned in. Louie was there to meet them.

"Got a sick horse? Must have eaten something that didn't agree with it," Louie observed.

"I guess that could be. Or maybe it's the heat. We've driven quite a few miles."

"You visitin' somebody out this way?" Louie asked, thinking maybe they were lost. He knew everyone for miles, and he'd never seen these folks.

"No, not really. My name is Carl Higgs. I started a law office in Wadena and am out to appraise an estate out this way. Thought it would be a nice ride for the Missus," he explained, casting a nervous eye toward the uncompromising woman in the buggy seat. She looked straight ahead in frigid silence.

Looking up at her with a smile, Louie suggested, "Better get in out of the heat, Ma'am. Lidy's likely got a cool drink about ready."

Ignoring the well-callused hand he held up to help her down, she favored him with a glance, saying, "No. No thank you. I'll wait right here."

"Up to you," Louie said over his shoulder, turning back to a horse definitely in pain. He'd noticed the woman wore a black dress of heavy material. Tight around her neck, long-sleeved, went way down to her heels. And a fancy hat.

Quickly, Louie unharnessed the horse, urging it toward the shade of a tree. "Startin' to bloat. Got colic, like as not."

"Hmmm. Didn't study that in law school. If you've got a phone I'll call a vet," Higgs said, casting ever more anxious looks at his wife's pink face.

"Nah. Don't need a vet for that, unless you particularly want one. I cure my horses when they get that. Usually works."

Another look at the woman in the buggy and the lawyer said, "Sure. Do what you do for your horses."

By this time, Lidy, who had been watching from behind a curtain, came out. With a wide smile, she went up to the buggy.

"Land sakes, you are going to get a stroke in this heat! I just made a pitcher of gingerale and our well is deep so the water is cold. Besides, you'll be sunburned to a crisp out here!"

It was the part about being sunburned that did it. Not waiting for a hand down, she got herself to the ground. Looking daggers at her man's back for letting his horse get sick, or asking her along, or whatever, she followed Lidy reluctantly into the kitchen. Louie called after them, "Ma, make some strong coffee. Real strong."

"This kind of weather is hard on the oats but good for the corn," Lidy offered by way of striking up a conversation. The woman obviously didn't give a rap about either. She stood in the middle of the kitchen with its scrubbed white board floor.

"Goodness, don't stop in the kitchen. We got comfortable chairs in here."

Lidy led the way into her parlor. Surely the new carpet with cabbage roses of dark red and wine, or the organ that reached almost to the ceiling, would get a word out of her. "You set down and I'll get us a cold drink." Lidy got the coffee ready, then went back in with tall glasses. The woman had chosen a straight, pressed back chair.

Louie got the coffee, cooled it down a bit, and funneled it into a long-necked green bottle he used to purge a sick animal when one needed it. The horse was down now, throwing its head and kicking its hind legs, with a belly so bloated it looked about to burst. Twisting its head sideways, Louie forced the bottle in behind its back teeth from the side and the coffee went down.

"There. If she ain't too bad, she should be on her feet again in an hour."

"An hour! Goodness me," Higgs said, looking at the back door.

Lidy tried valiantly to find something of interest to this miserable woman. What in tarnation *was* she interested in? Lidy had never known anyone not interested in anything! How sad, poor thing. She didn't make a sound at the picture Lidy showed her that Jen had just finished. She looked right past the Martha Washington geranium in bloom. She refused to have her glass refilled, and even kept her hat on!

Outside things were going better. Loud bursts of air were escaping from both ends of the horse. With each one its stomach shrunk a bit. The lawyer was saying, "Well, Louie, I'll be! Now whoever thought just coffee could do that! I'll pay you and then we'd best be on our way.

"I'd let it rest awhile yet. Been pretty sick, y'know. No charge. Anybody can get in trouble. Besides, I'd do it to help this animal if you was no place around!"

When the rig was driven up to the back step, the woman thanked Lidy in clipped tones. She was gracious

enough, but not friendly.

Several months went by, then one day the Gossell's had business in Wadena. Lidy needed several things in the drug store. She walked to the counter, surprised to find the person next to her was none other than the troubled Mrs. Higgs. Putting a hand on her arm, Lidy said, "Hello! We've often wondered how you folks got along. Got back to town all right, did you?"

Grabbing her purchases without recognition, Mrs. Higgs huffed her way out of the store.

"Takes all kinds," Lidy thought to herself.

Fifteen minutes later Lidy was going down the opposite side of the street toward where Louie had tied the buggy. There was no mistaking the tilt of her nose when the woman ahead of Lidy turned her head to look in a window. A hint of lace edging from beneath the woman's skirt drew Lidy's attention. Should she tell her? If so, how? The white strip was wider now, past the lace. Lidy knew how drawers were made – with a drawstring around the top that unless tied with care could come undone. Or break. Realizing she was in dire straits, the woman hobbled into the entry of a hardware store just before her pants fell in a heap around her feet.

Looking up to see how many had witnessed this terrible embarrassment, the woman saw Lidy.

"Oh, how unfortunate! Whatever should I do? I've never had this happen before. Help me. Lucy, isn't it?"

"Lidy. I guess if it was me, I'd step out of them pants and stick 'em in my hand bag. Who's to know if you've got any on or not?" Lidy suggested. Mrs. Higg's face was redder than the day out in the buggy. Now she grabbed Lidy's hand and thanked her profusely.

"Spread your skirt a bit and stand in front of me please," she said.

Lidy got in their buggy and, with a smile at Louie, they started home.

They were leaving the last houses of town behind when Lidy turned and said, "You know, Louie, there's just nothing that can bring a body down to common level like losin' your breeches on Main Street!"

Kate was a tiny woman. Too busy to "fuss," she wore her hair severely pulled back into a tight knot. Few remember having seen her without a floor-length dress, covered by an enveloping apron, and the battered black-cloth bag that held her medicines and the few instruments she used. While she was out doctoring or waiting for another brand-new citizen to "land", her husband waited on the customers in the drugstore. The Tarnows had several teenaged children, and the family lived in rooms in the back of the building.

Trained or not, Kate seemed to know what to do with the vials of pills and potions on the store's shelves. She concocted many of them herself, particularly the pink and blue pills and salves.

One old-timer remembers the pills as being the smallest things he had ever seen. "Drop one by candlelight and a feller could forget findin' it until morning-light," he said.

Another remembers that, when a baby brother got into a supply of pink pills, eating an unknown number of them, Kate soothed the distraught mother with "Never mind. Ain't anything in 'em, anyhow."

Kate had no transportation other than walking. Often, members of the ailing one's family came after her, then fetched her home again. She stayed until the patient was well or a more urgent case called her away.

The exact date the Tarnows moved to Hewitt is unclear, but it's agreed that they were established by the early or mid-1890s. Mr. Tarnow passed away while they lived in Hewitt and is buried in the oldest section of Mount Nebo Cemetery, along Highway 71, halfway between Hewitt and Wadena. The sons in the family kept the store going, so their mother could keep up her practice.

In the early 1900s, the drugstore was sold, and Kate

"Never give the blue pills with the blue salve. If you give the blue pills, you gotta use the pink salve. An' the other way around, too." That standard advice was almost always left with the patient before Kate Tarnow headed back to her drugstore in Hewitt, Minnesota.

As far as anyone ever found out, Kate had never so much as walked past a medical college. And, her background in pharmacy was debatable.

Yet, she is remembered by old timers in the Hewitt area as having an innate ability, somehow, to correctly diagnose most common ailments of that era as efficiently as a real doctor (few and far between). She was especially effective at a confinement case and was known for "pulling folks through," a particularly vicious brand of flu around the turn of the century.

went to live with one of her children in California, where she ultimately died.

About that same time, a bonafide doctor, with a brand-new license to prove it, by the name of Dr. George Lothian took up practice in the town. After several years in Hewitt, he went back to medical school and later earned the reputation of being one of the finest pioneer surgeons in the Midwest. He headed a hospital at Milbank, South Dakota, for many years.

Dr. Lothian's assessment of "Dr. Kate" was: "She did a remarkable job with what she had to work with. (Often onions were applied to the chest for congestion or to the feet to draw the blood away from the head in case of ear-ache.) She had an uncanny ability to correctly diagnose...then, do all she could about it." Kate also set many fractures that turned out fine.

Many are those, still in this area, who were ushered into the world with the help of "Dr. Kate's" gentle hands, and then were kept going by those pink and blue pills and salve.

The cover design of Donnelly's "Caesar's Column"

Early female impersonator was scandal of Minnesota!

Lucy Ann Lobdell's history began in 1855, Delaware County, New York. She lived among rough lumberjacks and hunters, who taught her everything they knew about the woods. Her hunting credits included a full-grown panther, 140 deer, 11 bears, and many wildcats, plus smaller game.

It was Lucy's skill with her rifle that was her undoing. A raftsman, named Henry Slater, made Lucy Ann a sporting proposition: Lucy and he would have a shooting match. If he won, she must become his bride. Though Lucy despised Henry, so sure was she of winning, she took him up on the wager.

Lucy lost.

Slater proved most undependable as a husband, and to escape him, Lucy Ann headed for Minnesota, dressed in men's clothes. She called herself "La Roi" Lobdell.

In St. Paul, Lucy made the acquaintance of Edwin Gribbel, who had no idea this person dressed in calico pants, vest and coat was a woman. For a time, "La Roi" and Gribbel lived on a claim near Lake Minnetonka, hunt-

ing by day and sleeping under the same blanket at night. Gribbel never found out the truth about his partner.

Lucy soon grew tired of waiting for the claim to be proved, and relinquished her rights to Gribbel for $75. She moved to Kandiyohi County, then on to Manannah in Meeker County.

There, in the summer of 1857, "La Roi" became a hired man. She did regular chores, chopped wood,

hunted and even washed dishes to pay for her board. She lived there a year before "Satan, with the air of original sin" discovered that she was an imposter.

When it was learned that "La Roi" was a woman, the Meeker County attorney filed suit against her, alleging that she falsely impersonated a man. This became a great scandal in Manannah, and against the peace and dignity of Minnesota.

When all was weighed, not enough evidence was found to convict her. It was not illegal to wear men's clothing on the frontier. Lucy was not punished in the courts, but she became the subject of harsh treatment. She became an outcast, then a public charge.

Lucy was sent back to New York a pauper. She ended up in Monroe County, Pennsylvania, living in a cave. There she subsisted on roots and berries, shunning civilization. Finally, after being arrested for a variety of small offences, such as vagrancy, she died. She was buried in Potter's Field.

If Lucy Ann Lobdell Slater, known as the "Wild Woman of Meeker County," hadn't been a crack shot, her story might have been different. Sadly, the shot that went wild, is the only one anyone ever heard tell of her missing.

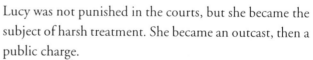

The wild goose chase of Sam Brown's crazy ride

Sam Brown of Brown's Valley, on the afternoon of April 19, 1866, rode all night and all the next day. Before he was done, he had covered 150 miles. It was entirely unnecessary. Brown didn't know it at the time. He thought it was up to him to save Dakota and Minnesota from an Indian uprising. This was only a few years after the Sioux Outbreak of 1862, and pioneers were inclined to be jumpy whenever the subject of Indians came up.

Sam Brown was the son of Major Joseph R. Brown, for whom Brown's Valley was named. He was also a celebrated scout and Indian fighter in the Dakota Territory and, at one time, was Indian agent in the district of Fort Wadsworth. One day information came to him that there was imminent danger of an Indian raid. A scout brought in word that Indian tracks had been discovered nearby, pointed toward the Minnesota territorial line. Fearing a bloody calamity, Brown set out to alarm the country and to warn other scouts to be on their guard.

Brown put on his buffalo-skin suit, saddled his best and toughest pony, and started for the Elm River scouting station sixty miles away. Let him describe his experience:

"I left about sundown and before I had gone very far darkness was upon me. The country was a wild, level plain, almost trackless, but on account of the darkness, I felt safe from ambush. The gait was terrific, both for horse and for me, but I dared not slacken the pace. About midnight I reached my destination, having covered the sixty miles in five hours. I immediately went to the chief of scouts and quickly explained matters, but imagine my mortification when he told me that there was no longer any danger of a raid; that the Indians who had been sent north as peace messengers must have been the ones whose tracks were seen in the vicinity of Fort Wadsworth."

All along the route Sam had aroused settlers, as well as sending a letter to St. Paul scout headquarters that there was going to be an invasion. He was embarrassed to return to Fort Wadsworth to quiet the alarm.

Sam procured a fresh pony for his ride home, and without resting, started back. He wrote:

"There was no moon and no stars. The north star peering through the clouds had guided me on the way over. There was nothing to chart my course but flashes of lightening. A storm was certainly coming. I tried to keep ahead of it by riding desperately. At breakneck speed my pony and I flew along over the James River flat, as level as a barn floor. In a few minutes the storm was upon me. It nearly unhorsed me, with rain, piercing and terrific.

"This soon turned to sleet and snow. Death was staring me in the face. The roar of the storm, the inky blackness of night, gave way to grim thoughts. Would I be lost or frozen? Waylaid or scalped, then left for the wolves? All thoughts combined terrified me. I managed, somehow, to keep the wind to my back and push on.

"My pony was tough and gamy. It galloped in driving rain, sleet, and snow, through slush and mud. Even swollen streams. Sometimes, it would slip and slide on frozen places, or break through soft ice and throw me in the water. This happened twice. Fortunately, I had fastened my hair lariat to the saddle, with the other end to my belt. At daybreak I saw I was at the foot of Coteau Hills and rode to the top. Now I found landmarks, Hawk's Nest and Buzzard's Roost. I knew I was twenty-five miles from the fort and fifteen miles from my route. I was shivering, cold to the bone, and all but given up. I gave the pony the rains. It jogged along at its own gait, picking its own way.

"I reached the agency at eight o'clock that morning, and rolled off the pony in a heap. It turned out that I'd gone 150 miles since I left the day before. I staggered to the stockade gate, falling headlong through the door of the house. I lay in a stupor for hours. When I regained consciousness, I told the commander to stop preparations.

"My great adventure had turned out to be a wild-goose chase, a false alarm."

Minnesota ghost ship haunts the lakes!

Most Minnesotans find themselves at one time or another standing on the docks at Lake Superior. We seem to be drawn to big water. Years ago, working on "the lakes" for a season was a fast way to make ends meet, to buy or pay for farms. An unpretty, but true, side of shipping out were the many ghost ships that did and still do inhabit her waters. These were ships that sailed from port with no problems, but never reached their destination, and often were never found or heard from again!

One such ship that met a sad ending was the Minneapolis. Her crew was made up mainly of Minnesotans from the Heartland trying to earn that bit of extra pay that would see them through. She is listed among the "phantom vessels."

The Minneapolis, loaded with lumber and shingles, headed out from the pier bound for Chicago. Her captain knew there was a disturbance on the Great Lakes, but it was a small one, far away, and Chicago was considered a short run. He believed a ship as tight and well-equipped as the Minneapolis could beat it. She was considered to be fast.

It was somewhere off the Apostle Islands in Wisconsin that the captain changed his mind. Suddenly the storm was upon him. Desperately, he decided his only recourse was to try to head back for the safety of the Duluth harbor. He finally got the ship turned, but during the minutes the vessel was in the trough of the seas, the entire deckload was swept away!

Floundering, pounding her way back toward the harbor, the captain was dumbfounded when no guiding lights appeared. He knew he was close, but where? He did not know that the lights had been swept out to sea by 35-foot waves. Suddenly, the Minneapolis struck bottom, sheared to starboard, and struck the north pier. Waves carried her back out where she broke in half. It is said that nine men in her crew had frozen to death a scant fourth-mile from the mainland. Most of her crew was made up of farmers from rural Minnesota trying to "make it."

Did you know that another ship, the Minnesota, played a vital part in the famous battle between the Monitor and the Merrimack? Well, it did.

The Minnesota was designed by the famous engineer and captain, John Ericcson. He was born in Vermland, Sweden, gravitated to England where he distinguished himself, then was lured to the United States. It was he who patented the first screw propeller, with most of the machinery below the water line. Also, his vessels were without smoking stacks to give them away.

On December 1, 1855, a brightly painted frigate slid into the chill waters of the Atlantic Ocean. Across her bow was printed the name "Minnesota." The president of the United States, Franklin Pierce, and his cabinet watched from the deck of the Engineer. Naval Department records tell us the ship was a wooden frigate, screw, first rate. Tonnage was 3,307 pounds, length 265 feet, with a beam of 23 feet. Her speed was nine and one-half knots per hour and she carried a crew of 540 men. She cost $691,409.00 and was equipped with the most sophisticated guns and cannons of the times.

The same Act of Congress that authorized the building of the Minnesota called for construction of another ship, the Merrimack. Later the Merrimack was taken over by the Confederate States and converted to an ironclad. The Minnesota rule-of-the-waves was short lived. She left Norfolk, Virginia, under the command of Captain S.D. DePont and cruised to Bombay, where her size put India's Chief of the Navy in shock. She went on to Muscat, where the Sultan himself came to verify rumors of her enormity.

The Frigate "Minnesota" (right) at Hampton Roads

Then, the Minnesota was called home.

Her next assignment: Hampton Roads, to assist older Union ships – the Congress and the Cumberland – in their fight against the ironclad Merrimack. Her 60-pounder breech loading rifle, 24 nine-inch smooth bores and 20-pounder guns were needed. At the end of the first day of fighting, the Congress was captured, the Cumberland sunk, and the Minnesota run aground. However, another ironclad, the Monitor, moving into the river channel under cover of darkness, used the Minnesota as a blind to take the Merrimack by surprise.

It was at Hampton Roads where the battle between the first ironclads in history took place – the Merrimack and the Monitor – on March 9, 1862. Bravely, before the Monitor was anywhere on the scene, the Minnesota pelted the Merrimack with all she had. But, the cannonballs from her biggest guns bounced off the armored Merrimack like marshmallows. Then, the Minnesota ran aground. Only the approach of darkness saved her. The next morning, the Merrimack leisurely returned to supposedly polish of the stranded Minnesota.

Not so! From the shadows behind the Minnesota a queer-looking craft emerged. Also designed by Captain John Ericcson, it was built low, with little superstructure exposed. Its name, the Monitor.

Neither ship could sink the other, but the warship Monitor saved the Minnesota. In 1867, the Minnesota was returned to service as a gunnery and training ship for naval apprentices to shoot at until October 18, 1895. The poor Minnesota was plastered with bullet and cannonball holes. Still, she simply would not go down.

Finally, in August 1901, she was stricken from the Navy Register and sold to a concern in Boston for $25,738.00. Only then did the Minnesota have to succumb to the torch in large, searing chunks.

She was never sunk. She refused to join the other victims that lay in the ignominious darkness of the ocean floor.

Black Plague memories haunt 90-year-old surviver of the prairie!

It was on May 15, 1875, that George stuck into his pocket Homestead Certificate Number 1054 for 160 acres of buffalo-prairie grass near North Platte, Nebraska, and headed for his 17' x 25' sod shanty. He was anxious to show it to Emmy and their six kids.

The Civil War was raging. Before George had time to make plans for his land, he was in uniform, headed south. Only old men, boys under fourteen, women and children were left to till the land, feed animals and take care of families.

Emmy was a buxom woman with a great sense of humor and a ready laugh. George knew that if any woman could, she would manage. All but the youngest three were crack shots. Indian raiding parties were very much in evidence. But it was not the Indians, however, that was the terror which was to devastate them beyond repair.

George had been gone three months when Emmy knew she was pregnant. Only a small fraction of letters sent from either direction reached their destination. Having Gramps, George's father, with them helped keep spirits up even though he was wracked with rheumatism.

Emmy scanned a sky clear of clouds. They needed rain. Bad! Dust sifted over everything, including the vittles. It was that morning that Carl, the oldest, said his throat hurt. He wouldn't eat. Emmy fixed Carl a glass of hot salt water to gargle with and told him to stay put for today. When they came in at noon from hoeing puny corn, he was hot to the touch and had a headache. He wheezed when he breathed.

A clatter of wagon wheels on a hard track came from the south. Gramps eased out of his chair to go out for a "howdy," as was the custom. Soon Gramps hobbled back inside, white around the mouth. When the kids were out of earshot, he said, "Jake says diphtheria has sprung up ever'where. The Ellis' already buried a kid."

Fear like an icy hand clutched Emmy's heart. She had been trying to push the awful thought away since yesterday morning. Carl's wheezing could be heard all over the shanty, coming faster now. He could no longer swallow.

Emily Harris

He looked up at her, grateful when Emmy put the corner of a rough huck towel soaked in cold water in his mouth. She cut large onions (set out early and big before the drought hit) all over the shanty. It was claimed they purified the air. By the next morning they had turned green. Folks said it was because they soaked up poisoned air. She replaced them each day with fresh ones.

But Carl couldn't be saved.

It was thus that Emmy's nightmare began.

Carl stopped wheezing abruptly the night of July 13th. Ira's throat was starting to swell shut and his eyes were big, knowing what had happened to Carl. Gramps alone chiseled a shallow grave from the beaten soil. Although there was trouble in every shanty, neighbors left boxes of staple groceries out by the road. A doctor of sorts stopped by with a lard-like salve. It did not help. A wooden leg kept Doc out of the army. When he could no longer handle seeing anymore grief, knowing he could do nothing, Doc embarked on a long, numbing drunk from which he never

let himself emerge.

Emmy desperately tried any cure she had heard of. Lard and turpentine rubbed on the chests of small victims covered with a wool cloth. Water and turpentine boiled on the stove. Kettles of water kept boiling around the clock.

Gramps made a place for Ira on July 17th. A bachelor on the next homestead, who claimed he was too old and ornery to die, took pity and came to help Emmy. He spelled her at sitting up nights. It was true, it seemed mostly children or the weak died. Nellie and John stopped eating about the same time. They died within two hours of each other on July 22nd.

Emmy's hair had turned white. She no longer spoke unless she had to. Little Sammy followed Nellie and John on August 3rd. Gramps, too, was heartbroken and exhausted. Emmy rocked Babe, the youngest and only one left, until she, too, faded away the eve of August 8th.

Emmy had lost six children in 23 days!

After Carl, things happened so fast Emmy could no longer cry. There was no emotion left. A hard lump in her chest was to never leave her as long as she lived, although she lived past her 75th birthday. Gramps' time also came that same year the children were lost.

Leaving with only a change of well-boiled clothing, Emmy moved to live with George's sister in North Platte to have her baby, now due. The shanty was burned to the ground with everything inside, like many others where plague had brought death and left stubborn germs.

George returned home with a gun-shot disability discharge that Emmy didn't know had happened. He found a tiny girl to welcome him in place of the six lively youngsters he'd expected. He hadn't had any news, either.

They moved to Grand Island.

That baby girl grew up, married, and moved to Wadena County in a covered wagon. It was also that baby, almost ninety years later, who told this story. She has no memory of ever receiving a kiss, a hug or even a smile from her mother. Emmy lost so much she never let herself love again.

Before his injury ultimately took his life, George managed to have six small graves and one big one moved to a regular cemetery in Grand Island where they can be found to this day.

Look for the name Harris.

True diary of black plague catastrophe in Minnesota

"Jan. 25: A new baby. Other children all sick but Prudy. Anna, Martha and John real bad. Doctor out from Doniphan (Nebraska). Left medicine. Don't seem to help much.

"Feb. 13: Anna died today. Martha and John worse, with Eva Alice almost as bad. Doctor from Lincoln today. Can't seem to stop it. Prudy too stubborn to take medicine. Steaming herself and chews cloves. Got to name the baby.

"Feb. 17: Today we laid little Martha beside Anna. God, when will this stop? Baby not acting good. Doctors say steam him. I am. John and Eva Alice are bad sick and William about the same. Can't we save none? Let the boys pick a name for the baby. John said, 'Name him William.' William said, 'Name him John.' We'll call him John William. More doctors and medicine today. Trying everything. Thank God for good neighbors Al and Dave, who stay right with us and help nurse. I don't think. Just work.

"Feb. 22: John and Eva Alice went today. Died fifteen minutes apart. Makes four new graves. Baby real sick and William not any better. William desperately bad. Said today, 'Mother, you didn't go to the cemetery with any of the rest of the kids. Will you go with me?' I promised.

"Feb. 28: Filled my promise to William. Watched them lay him side of Anna, Martha, John and Eva Alice. House seems so empty and baby and James still sick. Prudy still seems fine.

"Mar. 8: James was laid to rest. Lost six in twenty-three long days. Other children seem on the mend. Thank God."

By the time March 8th arrived, Emily Harris' dark hair had turned snowy white. Her mouth was a grim line that seldom let itself smile again for the rest of her life and, although her other children knew she loved them, she could never bring herself to outwardly show affection. She had been hurt too much.

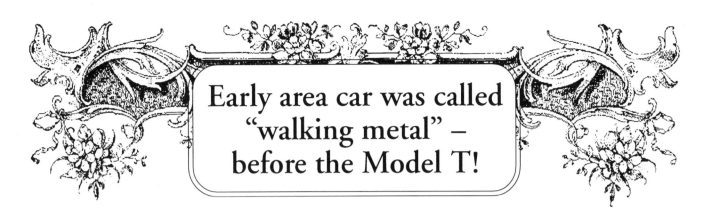

Early area car was called "walking metal" – before the Model T!

It was on July 4th, 1895, that Joseph Renshaw Brown, flushed with excitement, hurried to St. Paul directly to the levee. Today his friends and neighbors were going to see "Mazomanie" for the first time.

Mazomanie, meaning "walking metal" in Indian, was described in the paper Brown published at Henderson as "a machine that could run backward, turn around in a short space and carry many people."

Brown decided to demonstrate Mazomanie's potential after the fireworks that night. He bet a teamster with a team of Belgians that his machine could cross a creek first.

"Plunge ahead!" Brown yelled to his driver. "We can make 'er!" And Walking Metal wallowed in.

"More wood!" Brown shouted, since power depended upon steam. No matter how hard Mazomanie huffed and puffed it only mired deeper. It finally came to rest in the soft mud and heaved its last. It was later recovered and left to disintegrate at Fort Ridgeley.

FIRST FORD - This unpretentious car was the foundation which Henry Ford would build a billion dollar empire. It is truely the first Ford. It was known simply as the Model A Runabout.

LUXURY MODEL - The 1906-1907 Model K Ford. Designed for the rich market, it never sold well and is credited with being the basis for Ford's dislike for six-cylinder engines. The poor sales of this car, coupled with a similiar response on the earlier Model B, convinced Ford that the major automotive market would be in the lower priced cars. The quite successful models N-R-S (in the low price field) were produced concurrently with the Model K, and led to the development of the Model T.

A later, more successful relative of this first flivver was the Model "T" Ford.

Ed Myers was one of the first proud owners of such a vehicle. Like its counterparts, it refused to start in cold weather. Fortunately, Myers also owned some horses and had three sons. Each Fall, Myers instructed the boys to place the horse manure in a wide pile, with a ramp-like area on the side facing the road.

By the time cold weather struck, a respectable-sized pile of manure was ready. It was on this pile, headed toward the road, that father Myers wintered his flivver, with a robe throw over the hood. Myers' family usually made it

into town while neighbors drove teams or stayed home. They considered Myers "odd" to insist on wintering his precious automobile on, of all places, the manure pile!

However, father Myers reasoned that since fresh manure was added to the pile each day, it promoted the decomposition of horse manure, the chemical reaction of which gives off more heat than does any other animal waste. Enough, in fact, to keep the block of the Myers flivver from freezing except in the most extreme weather. He never explained his reasoning to anyone but his sons.

One day Sigverd Pearson (my father-in-law) treated a friend to a ride in his new 1915 Ford Model "T". After

the ride, Dad turned into his yard with a flourish and headed toward the house to park in its shade. As Dad slowed the car, the neighbor let out a yell filled with anguish. Dad pressed the brake harder only to be rewarded by a howl longer and louder than the first by his passenger.

Finally stopped, Dad turned to his friend, a bit peeved, saying, "What's the matter wit yew? I vas goint tew schtop! Yew tink I vould run down mine own heuse?"

No! No! But, Sigverd, mine sore big toe been under da schtopping petal!"

EARLY FORD - This 1909 Model T Touring featured windshield, top and lamps as options and this model does not have the windshield.

Minnesota nightmare in the lake of death

Ben came home from his job. He set his lunch pail down hard on the kitchen table. It was Friday. He was tired. He was heading for his easy chair when a happy idea struck him. Fishin'! Nothing took the tired out of a person's bones like fishin'.

The door slammed and Emma came in, face red from working the garden. How many times did he have to tell her not to work out there on a hot day? "How'd you like to go fishin', Em?" Ben already knew what her answer would be.

"Fishin'? Sounds good! I'll fix a lunch."

"Naw, lets eat a little now and just take coffee. We won't stay out late. It's the dark-of-the-moon tonight," he laughed, as if that made a difference. "I'll call Ed. Bet they'd like to go, too." Emma nodded. She liked Carrie.

An hour later found the four friends pulled up on the shores of their favorite lake. Years past, they'd each had a boat, but boats got old just like people and cost more for upkeep. Now they rented.

The men stopped by an office. "Not much left, boys. The fish are bitin' tonight, seems like."

"Hmmmn. Only two boats, huh? Makin' a choice shouldn't take long," Ed laughed, glancing at Ben. Ordinarily Ben liked a bigger boat, but they had used this size before.

In fifteen minutes they were ready. Ben watched as Em and Carrie settled themselves in the stern of the boat, already deep in conversation about the church bazaar. Those "girls" made pretty good-sized shadows these last years. Actually, they shouldn't be in the same end of the boat, Ben thought to himself, but he hated to spoil a good time. Besides, they weren't going far.

Ed teased the boat out carefully. There was almost no wind and in the twilight the lake looked like molten lead.

Ben caught a fish almost as soon as he wet a line. A ten-inch northern. He threw it back. Ed stopped the motor and threw a line in on the other side. The girls had stopped talking church stuff and already had pulled in a couple of little fellers. The fish were biting...but such tiny ones!

"Seems I saw a weed island out a little farther. Sometimes those lunkers like to lay on the bottom in a place like that. Must be a little shallower," Ben suggested.

Ed started the motor. "We'll just go up close to it. I'm not crazy about lake weeds. Gotta be careful."

It was dark now. You couldn't see where the lake stopped and the sky began. Ed pulled in the first five-pounder, and after that the rest landed fish as big or bigger. It was great! Em gave Carrie her favorite pickled-fish recipe. They watched the moon get more lopsided by the minutes, until only a thin slice remained. Soon, even that disappeared. It was dark! They couldn't see their own hands in front of their faces.

Ben was the first to say, "Better quit. We've got our limit and only kept the big ones. You girls can pickle all day tomorrow."

Ed started the Briggs and Stratton and they moved toward the lights on the shore. It sounded sluggish. Weeds on the propeller? He stopped and put the engine in reverse to unwind them if that was the problem.

Without warning, the boat went out from under them, stern first. There were four screams as the lake closed over their heads. Ben surfaced first. "Em, Em, where are you?" A body bumped his leg in the water. He reached down and gave a yank. He could hear her trying to get her breath. She had never learned to swim or even float.

From a short distance away, Ed called, "Hey, you guys, the boat has come up side of us! Bottom up, but it's floatin'!"

"Try to come toward my voice. I'll keep talking," Carrie gasped.

Ed and Carrie lived in a cabin on a lake at one time and were fair swimmers. Ben hadn't been in the lake for

years. Arthritis cut his swimming short.

"Don't think I'd try it. Distance fools a guy at night. Bill must be wondering where his boat is. He'll be out lookin' pretty soon," Ben reasoned. Another wave slapped, followed by a menacing "hsssssss." The boat settled another four or five inches.

Another long period of silence, and more insistent hsssssss's.

"Ben, I'm going to try it!" Ed said in a firm, tense voice. "I saw the lights in Bill's house go out two hours ago." Giving Carrie a cold, wet kiss, he turned and splashed away.

The moon was back to full power by now. They could see his head bobbing. He went about fifteen feet or so when there was a gasping, gargling sound, his hands stopped moving, his head disappeared!

All was quiet, except for the slap of the waves on what was still above the water. They knew Ed was gone! Soft sobs came from Carrie. Ben couldn't talk. Ed was his best friend. After a few minutes, Carrie said, "Hey, one of those flotation pillows washed up side of me. I-I think I can make it to shore with its help. It has arm straps."

"No! No, Carrie! We don't want to lose you, too. Please, don't try it! Most of the lights are out on shore now. You'll go the wrong direction," Ben begged.

"No, no I won't. Besides, without Ed life isn't worth much to me anyhow." Neither family had had children, which played a part in drawing them together. She said, "Pray for me," and shoved off.

Now they were alone. Ben silently cussed himself with words he hadn't learned in church. Three mistakes! Three bad mistakes! And by a man his age who'd spent as much time in a boat as he had over the years. It was unforgivable! He'd known the boat was too small, but he hadn't said so. He'd not mentioned it when the girls both sat in one end of the boat. Worst, he hadn't handed out the life preservers from their compartments. The lake had been so smooth. They wouldn't be going out far. Did a person ever learn not to go against their better judgment? Evidently not him.

Em had always known what he was thinking. Now she laid a hand on his shoulder. "Don't blame yourself, honeybunch," she said.

"Keep your hands on the boat!" he snapped. She started to cry.

After what seemed a long time, Em quavered, "B-Ben, the water is over my lap. The-the boat is sinking, isn't it?"

"Goin' down some, I guess. But there's air chambers built into the side of this boat. Shouldn't go down much farther. Not for a long time anyhow." He wished he believed himself. He'd hoped she wouldn't notice how fast air was escaping. He couldn't feel his hold on the boat anymore. He'd managed to kick off his shoes, which helped a lot.

What seemed like a lifetime went by. To break the monotony, Ben suggested, "We should be singin' 'Old MacDonald Bought The Farm,' or 'Rock of Ages.' That's what they sung when the Leviathan was goin' down, didn't they? In books people sing when they are in a jam."

"Don't!" Now it was her turn to snap. "Do you think she made it?"

"Could be. The wind is in her favor."

Another quiet spell, each in his own terrified thoughts. Ben guessed it to be around 3 a.m. by the look of the moon. "'I-I hear something. Do you?" Em asked hopefully.

"Likely a plane heading for the Bemidji field." He didn't want her to get her hopes up for nothing. All he could hear was water.

"No, l-listen!" At the same time a powerful light stabbed the darkness, sweeping back and forth over the lake. Not realizing it couldn't be heard over the motor, they yelled with what strength they had left. Ben said, "Wave your arm above your head!"

The sound headed their general direction. The beam of light swept past...then swung back to settle on them.

Ten minutes later found them being helped out of the Sheriff's rescue boat and into a waiting ambulance with warmed blankets. Ten minutes after that, they were already in clean, warm beds that felt heavenly! Carrie, they were assured, was sound asleep in the next room, exhausted, but all right. After bringing a cup of hot chicken soup and tucking them in, the nurse reached to switch off the light.

"Please leave all the lights on!" Em pleaded.

She did.

Women revile the cowardly men as Wadena burns to the ground

These buildings had a narrow escape. They were adjacent to the block that burned. Aldrich Avenue South East

This is an actual historic account as reported in the August 13, 1888, *Wadena Pioneer Journal:*

At fifteen minutes of one o'clock last Monday morning Marshal Carroll discovered fire in the rear of the vacant building on Third Street, formerly occupied by L.L. Benedict as a drug store. When discovered the fire was confined to a very small space and gave very little evidence of the damage to be accomplished in a few short hours. The fire was evidently caused by kerosene oil, for when water was dashed upon it the flames spread with great rapidity. Seeing that the fire was beyond his control, he hastened to give the alarm by ringing the fire bell. The Wadena fire department responded in a very few minutes and manned the apparatus at the reservoir on Front Street. Only by the most persistent effort was it possible to pro-

cure enough men to handle the engine, the great majority preferring to stand around, look at the fire and boss the department.

Notwithstanding all of this, the boys went to work with a will and soon had the flames pretty well under control. At this time the water supply failed and it became necessary to shift the engine to the well on Third Street. By this time the fire had gained considerable headway but by hard work the flames were again almost quenched. At this point the water supply was exhausted for the second time. An attempt was then made to get water from the well farther up Third Street but the hose was too short by several hundred feet. The same difficulty was experienced when an attempt was made to procure water from the railroad tank. As water could not be procured an effort was then made

The Merchant's Hotel

to tear down the Thorp & Ostrander's office and Kramer's millinery store, thinking by this means to let the fire exhaust itself.

The men worked with a will but the flames spread with such rapidity that they were soon driven from their post. The flames speedily communicated to the Ostrander building on the north and Montgomery's machinery hall on the south. It now became evident that the entire block would most likely go and the attention of those present was directed towards removing what loose property the buildings contained. On the south side the fire rapidly spread to Palmateer's barber shop, Mrs. L. Kramer's millinery store, Oscar Weickert's meat market, Green & Weeks' hardware store, the dwelling occupied by M. Davison, and Mrs. M.J. Potter's restaurant. Here the fire was checked simply because of lack of any more material.

On the north the flames quickly communicated with the Wadena Exchange Bank. To this was attached the building owned by J.J. Meyer and occupied by Meyer & Coon as a general store. Both buildings burned with great rapidity. From here the fire spread west along Front Street, burning the Gem Saloon, occupied by H.M. Dibble, a

vacant store building owned by W.R. Baumbach, and the post office building owned by L.E. Stinehour. It now looked like a clean sweep for the whole block, the Merchant's Hotel, a fine three story structure, and

FRONT STREET - NORTH						
Merchant's Hotel	L.E. Stinehour	Post Office	Vacant Store	Alley Way	Gem Saloon	Meyer & Coon General Store
						Wadena Ex. Bank
Vacant Lot	Potter's Restaurant	Thorp & Ostrander				
		Drug Store				
		Machinery Hall				
		Dwelling & Barber Shop				
		Millinery Store				
		Meat Market				
		Green & Weeks				
		Residence				
AVERILL AVENUE						

AVERILL AVENUE -- BRYANT AVENUE SOUTH EAST

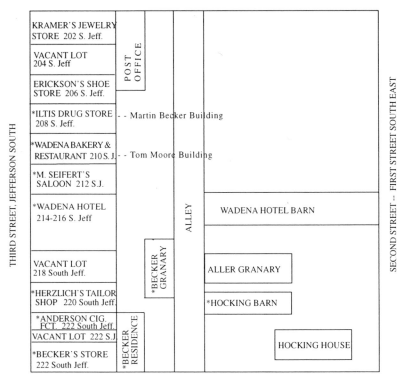

KING AVENUE -- COLFAX AVENUE SOUTH EAST

Fire in the 202 South Jefferson block on April 5, 1897
as reported in the Wadena County Pioneer of April 9, 1897

*identifies building destroyed
Drawn November 25, 1995, R.C. Zosel

out about half of his stock. Those burned out complained that a great deal of their property was stolen during the fire. Vandals who commit such mean, contemptible tricks out to be shot on the spot. The ladies put to shame a score of dudes who were too nice to help and when the men at the pumps became exhausted the women took their place. To them belongs the credit of saving the Merchant's Hotel and Stinehour's building. The lazy galoots who stood around with their hands in their pockets during the fire ought to be drummed out of town. Any person who will see men working the pumps when they are ready to drop to exhaustion, and who will see women endangering their lives and health in an endeavor to save property, do not deserve the title of men. This will touch a lot of persons in a tender spot but we cannot help it.

Stinehour's notions store being the only two buildings left in the block. At this time it was discovered that the hose would reach the two latter buildings from the N.P. reservoir. By almost superhuman efforts the fire was now confined to the burned district, the ladies helping man the pump. Although the Stinehour building caught fire half a dozen different times it was quickly put out and the worst was soon over. When it is considered that only fifteen feet separated the post office and Stinehour building, and that they were connected by a porch, the effectiveness of the department ought to be patent to all.

On the east side of Third Street the buildings were badly scorched. The plate glass windows all ruined. Several buildings caught fire but it was quickly put out. Burch moved

STRAY EMBERS:

Some contemptible sneak stole $12.00 from Mrs. Potter while her household goods were being moved.

One woman was observed wringing her hands and giving vent to loud lamentations. A sympathetic neighbor approached her and asked her if she had lost all of her possessions in the fire. No, they had all been saved, but she was afraid her poor dear husband would work too hard.

CARD OF THANKS:

The sufferers by the fire Sunday night desire to express to the fire department of Wadena most hearty and appreciative thanks for the persevering labor and zeal so heroically manifested during the burning of sixteen buildings, the water supply failing before thirty minutes had elapsed. All honor to the brave men who thus risk health and life

A brick building that replaced one of the wooden ones that burned. Proud owners stand in front.

itself, for the lives and property of others, receiving no compensation but fault finding and jeers for not doing more. To the citizens, not the members of the fire department, who did equally as good and efficient work, and to the strangers in our midst, we extend grateful thanks.

Last, but by no means least, we will with ever grateful hearts remember the noble women, young and old, who, seemingly endowed with superhuman strength, carried loads too heavy for men, passed and carried water, and when the foreman of the engine appealed in vain for men for more strength on the pump, sprang forward with willing feet and steady hands and saved for us the Merchant's Hotel, of which we are so justly proud; also the store of L.E. Stinehour. May the noble conduct of the women of Wadena put to blush the strong able bodied men who stood with callous hearts and idle hands because the fire (the light of which brought out into repulsive ugliness their selfish natures) was no funeral of theirs.

Strange tale of the grasshopper holocaust

Near Cold Spring, Minnesota, setting high on a hill you will find a tiny chapel probably not as large as your own living room.

It consummates a pledge made by the good farmers of that area a hundred years ago.

The season was ideal, that spring of 1876, with hopes high. Young crops flaunted a growing shade of green partial to Minnesota this time of year. Cattle wintered well and June grass elbowed sweet white clover for growing space in the pastures.

Best of all was the wheat. Already knee high. It was here, with the wheat, the farmers' hopes were tied.

In the wake of the Civil War, railroads pushed further west in search of food as the wheat fields of the middle west stretched east to meet them.

Money from wheat paid off mortgages; built warm houses and barns, bought more land. Little did the people of Cold Spring know that before night fell in their placid little community they would be in the midst of a plague equally as terrible as that described in Joel of the Old Testament.

On this particular bright June day in 1876, a haze that became a dark cloud obscured the sun. Seconds later it descended in a whirring, scratching, blurring scathe of wings upon the farmers and every other thing, living or not.

No mere grasshoppers, these!

They were huge, ugly things with fat bodies three inches long. Eyes as large as the top of a shingle nail on heads like the end of your little finger that worked back and forth in a swinging, mowing motion as they ravaged everything edible in sight, plus some items never meant for food.

They were not natives of this flat region but Rocky Mountain locusts, more commonly called "choppers".

The tender stalks of young wheat went first, along with the farmers' hopes. Then the pastures, gardens, and leaves off the trees disappeared in fast order.

Next, these creatures of the devil with the voracious appetites devoured clothing off farm wives' clotheslines, plopped by sickening hundreds into the water supply, and even worked their way into the houses.

They chewed great holes through the hides of the farm animals to the extent where many of them had to be shot. Darkness seemed only to whet their rapacious habits and it is said that their insatiable jaws could actually be heard working.

Since choppers had struck four times before; in 1856, 1865, 1873, and 1874, this pestilence was not new. Never, however, had its disaster reached such proportions.

Banding together, the farmers dragged great sheets of tin covered with tar after themselves in the fields, now no more than black stretches of naked earth. After the first few minutes, enough choppers were embedded in the tar so that the rest went merrily over the top.

Every means to combat them that came to mind was used. Farmers fashioned bulky nets at the end of long sticks to swoop them up. They tried burning, but not enough vegetation was left to burn.

Oil was spread and set ablaze. This was slow, hot work that a small percentage of the pests were caught by. The Stearns County Board voted to offer bounties for the choppers and their smeary yellow eggs that covered every available surface.

They paid for them **by the bushel**!

At last the winter in Minnesota settled down with its icy blasts and the farmers gave a great collective sigh of relief. True, feed was in such short supply as to be non-

existent, so most of the animals had gone to market, but surely, temperatures that ranged in the thirty-below zero mark for several months would prove too much for the pesky choppers, they thought.

Spring never comes slowly in Minnesota. It lands solidly on both feet, seemingly overnight. The spring of 1877 was no exception and, to see the trees, roadsides, and pastures coming forth with new untainted green despite the terrible purge of the last summer, lifted each farmer's spirits as he planted new wheat; new hope.

The first sign of the choppers came as a multitude of tiny winged things one-third the size of a housefly that flew or hopped faster than a man's eye could follow them. With sinking hearts the farmers realized the growing year of 1877 was to be as doomed as the preceding one. Farmers stood in groups of three or four on the corners in Cold Spring and neighboring towns, a story of gloom and despair written on haggard faces.

Financially broken, stymied in every direction, the good people surrounding the little quarry towns turned to their last hope; prayer.

Besides donating a reported $10,000 of his own money, Governor John E. Pillsbury cemented their efforts by setting aside April 26, 1877, for prayer and fasting.

Being almost entirely Catholic, the people promised, "Mother of God, rid us of this pest and we will build a chapel to offer up prayers of thanksgiving for thy goodness."

A high hill at the edge of town, topped by beautiful trees, was chosen as the site and a tiny edifice 16'x26' was built of timber. A statue of the Blessed Mother and Child carved by a local farmer graced the altar. This pocket-sized sanctuary was the 801st church in Minnesota, according to available records.

In 1893, the chapel was turned into a pile of twisted rubble by a tornado. Only the statue, buried at the bottom of the mess, could be salvaged.

The statue was stored and the rebuilding of the chapel lived only in the minds of men until the summer of 1952, when Bishop Peter W. Bartholome of St. Cloud, Minne-

sota, revived the issue by turning actual construction plans over to Reverend Victor Bonellenfitsch, pastor at Cold Spring.

Now it stands once more, built on the original footing, constructed of lovely, durable granite so plentiful everywhere in this area, only twenty miles from St. Cloud, Granite Capitol of the World.

The Blessed Mother and Child again presides at the altar and the doors are never locked against those in earnest search of meditation and prayer.

It is officially called Assumption Chapel and on each August 15th, the Bishop of St. Cloud offers solemn pontifical mass to the Blessed Virgin for favors of the past years.

On that morning the hillside teams with grateful people from all points in Minnesota as well as many other parts of our nation.

Believe as you will, it cannot be denied that on August 15, 1877, four months after the chapel was built and dedicated to prayer, for some mysterious reason, those winged emissaries of the devil arose as one into the sky and flew back from whence they came.

Not once in the intervening hundred years have the choppers returned.

If there is another answer, based on cold logic, aside from the one they found in the chapel the choppers caused to be built, the people of Cold Spring haven't heard it.

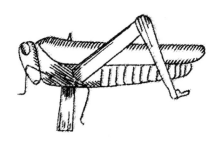

The Dude
of Wadsworth Trail

Refinement and elegance arrived at Gager's Station, located on the Wadsworth Trail (a few miles north of Morris, Minnesota) at the same time. One was driving the other.

The epitome of refinement was Albert Hawkes, driving a team of oxen so elegant they did not respond to ordinary commands.

Hawkes had played in a famous orchestra in the East, and had come West for an adventure. He was always pleasant and courteous, his clothing the cleanest of any in the crowd. And, as though that were not enough, nothing could provoke him to drink, smoke, cuss or gamble.

Only an ever-abiding sense of humor, that kept those around him doubled-up with laughter, saved a sterling character from being the butt of many a crude joke.

Hawkes looked over a number of oxen teams before heading West. All were such common beasts, understanding only "hish", "gee" and "haw". He elected, instead, to buy a young pair of oxen and train them himself.

Hawkes loved to square dance, and this team would be a constant reminder, he vowed, of all the good times (and girls!) he had left behind.

Nobody knows how long it took Hawkes to teach his oxen to respond to "Forward all", "Promenade", "Gents to the right", or "Swing your partners" – each of which was a definite command.

He had a charming voice, suited for outdoor calling, and nobody within earshot could keep a straight face when

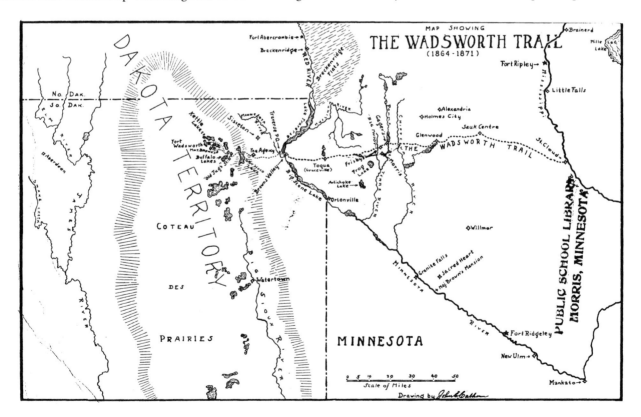

The Wadsworth Trail, Morris, MN

those lumbering oxen obeyed such frivolous directions as "Ladies forward and back", or "Allemande left"!

When Shanghai Chandler, Morris newspaperman, heard of it, he laughed heartily, saying: "Such calls are improper and entirely out of place. The man should be arrested. The idea," he whooped, "of shouting to an ox with a crumpled horn, 'Allemande left'! All wrong. All wrong and wicked," he'd gasp, wiping tears of laughter from his eyes.

Hawkes went from Gager's Station to Bismarck, North Dakota, and drove the stage from Bismarck to the Black Hills, over a newly laid trail. Soon after, he was one of the first drivers to be shot by Indians on that trail.

According to history, the portion of trail from Gager's Station to Bismarck was a teamster's nightmare and an Indian's paradise.

In places, it bogged out of sight into mud and sinkholes, often causing three-ton loads to be unloaded, then loaded again and taken across in short hauls. The terrain was sometimes covered with dense, concealing brush.

Other times it crossed the tops of hills, putting teamsters in full sight of anyone for miles, a perfect target. Young Indian bucks thought it great sport to hide in ambush, then suddenly jump from cover to clamber over a lumbering supply train in search of guns, ammunition, whiskey, tobacco, sugar, salt, molasses or coffee – in that order of preference.

Should the supply train be loaded instead with blankets, mail, hardware supplies or anything the Indians could not use, the hapless drivers often paid with their lives,

brutally beaten by the furious bucks.

The blood of Albert Hawkes and his compatriots kept open a trail that had to be traveled if the West was to be won.

Thus ends the story of one fine spirit in the new West. Happily, stories of the refined Albert Hawkes and his unusual team of oxen live on – to be revived now and again for yet another smile.

RIGHT:
Wadsworth Trail Barn, Morris

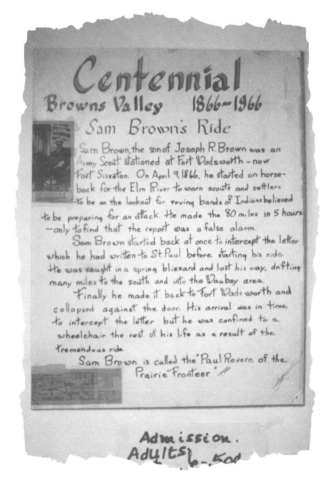

Centennial
Browns Valley 1866 ~ 1866
The Log House ~ Brown Museum

Log House 12

The Bronze Plaque

Former Picket Fence

Brown Museum ~ Now

The Log House was built in the vicinity of Fort Wadsworth, now known as Fort Sisseton. The oak logs were cut from the trees in the nearby ravines.

In 1866 it was dismantled and moved to Browns Valley where it served Joseph R. Brown and his family as a trading post and as a dwelling.

In 1871, a year after Joseph R. Brown's death, the house was taken down. All logs were marked. These were moved across the Little Minnesota River by ox team.

It was then rebuilt at the present location exactly as it had been originally. The bronze plaque was placed there later under the direction of Wm. L. Paal. The Flag Pole is a recent addition.

The Log House ~ Brown Museum

Joe Rolette. The drivers of the Red River carts wore sashes like the one in the picture.

The Stone

The stone ... Lake Traverse near the Islands. It was found in 1934, when Lake Traverse was dry. The markings of the cross are likely the result of erosian. The texture of the pinker stone is finer and probably harder.

The stone and its cross was evidently a grave marker. A double row of stones outlined the grave and a complete skeleton was found there.

Lake Traverse was totally dry in 1934, too; the grave could have been dug and marked by the stone at that time. This could have been the grave of an early Christian, white or Indian. This, too, is one of the mysteries of Lake Traverse!

In a Museum of the Minnesota Historical Society is a Red River cart that looks like this picture.

The dynamite blasters of Detroit Lakes!

Worth Hosmer was born to Burt and Alma Hosmer on July 2, 1896, at Janesville. His grandfather, for whom he was named, was a pioneer storekeeper. Burt kept bees. He found that by moving slowly he seldom got stung. He sold many thousands of pounds of honey each year.

There were five boys and two girls. Worth landed fourth from the oldest.

In 1902 Burt moved his family to Jeffers, twelve miles north of Windom, where he had three hundred fifty acres of good land and a fair-sized herd of cows. In 1915 the family moved to a farm at Eagle Bend. Worth and Bessie Konkle were married in Long Prairie.

After farming for one year, Worth and his brother Gene bought a used Sparta well-drilling rig for $700. Worth figured right from the start that it would be a good venture. Ask anyone what is of most importance to both man and beast the year round? Water, of course. It was the recognition of this need, along with the desire to help his fellow man, that prompted Worth and Gene to become proficient drillers of wells.

It was an exceptionally dry year in 1942, with wells going dry faster than they could be dug. Farmers were frantic for water. The Hosmer rig could go down 300 feet or more, which was usually more than enough. Most wells ran from 60 to 80 feet deep. The charge was $1.80 per foot.

Water-witching? You bet! Worth said it paid off more times than not. He liked to cut a water wand from a hazel bush that had a fork. It had to be supple and green.

The boys worked from daylight until dark; water was so important. A horse and buggy was driven to work each day and they were fed by the family they worked for. In most places, meals were good. They had very little trouble

getting their pay, though they had to wait a few months sometimes. Worth and Gene worked together for many years, until Gene bought Worth out and headed to Detroit Lakes with the rig, where he was still drilling wells at age 81!

Things have changed a lot. Then there was only solid tools, which had to be pounded sharp again after hitting so many rocks, of which there were plenty. Tall tripods, ropes and pulleys were standard equipment.

The only close call Worth had, other than skinned knuckles, was the time he was standing under a heavy pulley that broke loose high above his head. He heard shouts and threw himself sideways.

"Only got a busted leg out of it," he recalled.

Worth lived on their farm until 1958, when he moved into Eagle Bend. He continued fixing pumps and wells for people. Bessie passed away in 1972. A granddaughter he adored, Jeanne Simar, helped Worth after that.

Worth started chuckling. He felt a story coming on.

"There was this fellow, see? By the name of Lew Allen. He was so anxious for water he hardly got out of our way. Got a box and set on it right close. We got down 30 or 40 feet an' hit a rock. A big one. Gene decided he was gonna bust that rock if it took this – an' he held up 21 sticks of dynamite, lighted them, and dropped them down that hole.

"Now, I tell you, when THAT charge went off the ground shook like jelly! A spout of dirt went into the air 30 feet. The jolt knocked cream cans off a porch 50 feet away. The fellow who was so interested just rolled off his box sideways and started crawlin' without a word. Last we saw of him he was goin' lickety-split over the hill, still on his hands and knees. We laughed until we were about

sick. Oh, yeah! It busted the rock all right. We got all kinds of good water."

Worth agreed that his name was an unusual one. Other than the grandfather he'd been named after, he had run into only one other fellow with that name, also a well-driller, down by Little Falls.

"Would you believe," Worth asked between chuckles, "that poor cuss's last name was 'More'?" Worth and I spent the next ten minutes commiserating with that little boy of long ago and what he must have suffered at the hands of schoolmates and all the rest of his life. What a sense of humor those pioneer parents must have had, if not short on consideration, to name a child that.

"What d'you bet they didn't name the last one 'Noah'?" Worth inquired. This is too much! We whooped until tears streamed down our faces. I couldn't see my pencil.

After intense effort, we got back on a more serious vein, and Worth told me he believed the "Soil and Water" men when they claimed pure water is harder to find each year, what with so much poison run-off from fields.

"We're killing ourselves," he claimed. "You know there's many underground rivers running every which-way that carry poisons for miles, even into the next state."

At 86, Worth maintained that if he were young again, he would be a well-driller. Besides the joy of giving a neighbor cool, clear water for his family and stock, there was always the element of surprise – where would they find the best place to drill for water? How deep down would it be? Would it be good water? Lots of things.

Yessir, it was a mighty satisfyin' life and he'd sure go do it again.

The torn and mutilated victim who learned to live without complaint!

Fred "Frank" Arendt

Six-year-old Frank lay in the grass side of two dusty wagon tracks. Panic stricken. His right leg lay twisted beneath him at a funny angle. Blood seeped through his pants and ran down his leg. He didn't cry until he saw Pa running the horses down the road toward town. That's all he remembers.

What seemed like hours later, Frank heard a strange voice saying, ". . . lost alotta blood, too. An' he's plenty puny anyhow. I'll do what I can."

"It happened so fast, doc! I allus told the kids to be careful of gettin' a leg in a wagon wheel!"

Frank awoke in his own bed. Something didn't feel right. It was then he noticed one leg had been amputated above the knee. Ma looked worried. Pa was cryin'. Two older brothers looked on, big-eyed.

The stump finally healed and Frank began experimenting with wood shaved to what was left of his leg. By the time he was fourteen he'd fashioned a contraption, padded on top, with leather straps that held it in place enough so he could walk. He had good balance. Now he could follow behind his brothers outside without hopping.

Just losing a leg would have been enough, but when he was a baby Frank had polio or some darn thing that stunted his left arm and limited the use of that hand. However, nothing dampened an enduring sense of humor. When anyone sympathized, he answered, "It coulda been worse. At least my gimpy arm an' peg leg ain't on the same side."

Frank claims it was most disgusting when he didn't stop growing until he was six foot, four inches! Wouldn't ya know it? His brothers were much shorter. "Kept me whittlin' on my next leg every rainy day, just to stay level.

An' when I out-growed one, well, how'd you like to see your ma throw one of *your* legs in the stove?"

Frank learned to be a good shot with one hand. One Sunday afternoon he and his brothers were target shooting at a tin can on a rock. When he stood to one side, waiting his turn, a bullet hit the rock, ricochetted, and put out one of his eyes. Now, wasn't *that* the very devil?

Frank and one of his brothers farmed together after their folks died. The other brother was also dead. With one good hand, one leg and one eye, Frank claims he could do almost anything his brother could. So, you see, it coulda been worse.

Ten years later Frank and his brother were putting up meadow hay with a homemade stacker. It was their own invention. It went up into the air with a two-by-four level six feet long that they pulled to release a sling of hay when it had reached the desired spot from the top of three long poles tied teepee-style over the stack.

It was Frank's job to man the lever while his brother yelled from the other side of the stack when to pull. Frank didn't hear the command to "Let 'er go!" When he came to, he started to spit out blood and teeth before he discovered it had hit him with such a whallop it broke both jaw bones! They swung like a garden gate.

Go to a doctor? Not on your life! Not with all he had wrong already. Besides, in time bones healed on their own, didn't they?

Frank's jaw bones didn't. He called them his "free-wheeling jaw" an' not many people had one, he bragged. By hunching one shoulder high, he could eat soft things. To talk, he used his good hand to stabilize his mouth.

Next, Frank's brother died, leaving him alone in their three-room shack. He sold what livestock and machinery they had and was contemplating what he should do when one winter night his shack burned down. Taking everything he owned with it. Even his dog. It paid to sleep in your clothes, like he'd been doing the last years.

The social services worker for his county came that same night and put him in her car and headed for a nursing home.

When the social services worker commiserated with Frank on his almost unbelievable amount of tragedy and bad luck, Frank looked at her with his good eye, put a hand to steady that free-wheeling jaw, and with the semblance of a grin declared, "It coulda been a lot worse. I coulda got married!"

Author Ethelyn Pearson was the woman who checked "Frank" in at the nursing home and did a preliminary history on him. She said he was covered with smoke and soot, was filthy and very hungry. "He was fed even before the nurses started cleaning him up," she said. "His woolen underwear had to actually be peeled off. He'd cut his own hair."

"Frank" was in his early 70s and Pearson said he was a "delight" to both staff and residents.

"He was always cheerful and found a bright side to everything," she said. "I asked for the job of outfitting him with new clothes and chose flannel shirts in bright red or blue plaids. He loved them. He cut the right leg off all the new pants before wearing them so his peg would show. His mouth was in terrible shape, but he refused dental work, as well as a natural-looking leg. 'I couldn't desert my old leg now, not after it has held me up all these years and got me out of that house on fire. What would it think of me?' he said."

"Frank" lived in the nursing home for the next seven years. Pearson said he soon became a favorite among other residents and he tried to lighten their lives by describing some way things "coulda been worse."

One night "Frank", who was in his mid-80s, bid his roommate a "Goodnight, an' don't let the bedbugs bite," as he usually did, then crawled into his bed, pulled up the blankets and fell into what was to be his last sleep without an ache or pain. Pearson came to work the next morning and found that he had died in his sleep.

"I'd learned to love the old guy,'" she said, "and couldn't help shedding a quiet tear, thanking God for making his death so painless. I could just hear 'Frank' saying, 'It coulda been worse.'"

The lost art of farm-to-farm selling in old Minnesota

Little did the jeweler realize that a nationwide mail-order empire, still in business into its second century today, would be inspired when he refused a shipment of watches he had not ordered.

The year was 1881; the place, Redwood Falls, Minnesota. An eighteen-year-old fellow named Richard Warren Sears was the depot agent there besides acting as postmaster and running a store on the side. The combination of jobs gave Sears the inside track on things sometimes, like when the watches were returned.

Sears had helped support his family since he was seven, when he carried water to field hands for 25 cents per day. Richard's father, James, came back from the Civil War with a wounded leg and what was described as a distraught nature. As his father withdrew more and more into himself and away from his family, his wife, Eliza, devoted more and more attention to her oldest son and mainstay, who was Richard.

Sears was born December 7, 1863 at Stillwater. His father was a blacksmith and the family moved often. Although he had very little schooling, a strong sense of business acumen was evident in young Sears, and he never passed up a chance to learn. At the age of sixteen, he knew telegraphy and was appointed depot agent at Wolsey and Mitchell, South Dakota, Minneapolis and North Redwood.

Sears got the unclaimed shipment of watches for half-price and sold them for five dollars apiece. Working for the railroad made it possible for him to travel wherever the rails were laid. This meant most of Minnesota, including Detroit Lakes, Park Rapids, Wadena, Staples, Fergus Falls and many other places. Sears' sales pitch was "No money needed." He was always honest and gave full value. Since it was imperative that he keep his job, he made good use of vacation time and whenever else he could.

Sears' long association with farm families and poverty gave Sears an uncanny talent for analyzing what a farm family would want, and what they could pay. About this time, railroads began to spread, carrying mail to remote areas and it occurred to him that his time was worth more than postage would be.

Sears quit railroading and with fifty dollars established a business in Chicago in 1886. There he ran an ad for a watch repairman, which was answered by Alvah Curtis Roebuck. The two men hit it off immediately and Roebuck bought into the company.

Many new lines of merchandise were added to the watches and jewelry, such as groceries, a car called The Sears Buggy that sold for $525 and patent medicines. The medicines were top sellers, including such items as Dr. William's Quick Cure for Indigestion and Dyspepsia, Brown's Vegetable Cure for Female Weakness, Wonder Heart Cure, Service Cure for Tobacco Habit and Dr. Hammond's Internal Catarrh Cure, along with many more.

Sears had a flair for writing appealing copy and the first huge shipment of catalogs went out in the fall of 1887. Sears sold the business (the first of two times, as he bought it back later) to Roebuck when he was twenty-five years old.

During the years of his selling, Sears established a creed for the company that prevails to this day: never argue with a customer over anything, as a satisfied customer means a customer who will return and buy much more than was lost by the company, even if the company was right. He

made sure as much as was possible that all of his employees followed this rule.

Until the day he died, on September 28, 1914, Sears was friendly, honest, a devoted son and husband. He made for himself a special place in the hearts of country folk, his favorite people, who always welcomed his wide smile and friendly ways. His next visits were looked forward to

as he was invited to shove his knees under many a farm wife's table come mealtime. He always left something for the kitchen from some of his wares.

A favorite quote of Sears was, "He who sits atop the heap can afford to banish ill will and to harbor only magnanimity."

No meteorologists were there to warn pioneers of deadly hail!

In 1853 a man named Collins landed in Eden Prairie just in time to find a lynch court in session, hardly a passive scene. Previous descriptions led him to expect to find Eden Prairie a place where there were friendly people who would help him, where a Christian attitude went without the saying. It seemed that a certain Mr. Gorman had squatted on a desirable passel of land that squatter Samuel Mitchell also wanted. Both men being Irish, with Gorman a Catholic and Mitchell a Protestant, didn't help a whole lot. Gorman filling Mitchell's left arm full of shot did nothing to ease the situation for Gorman, who was then ordered to leave town with his family within twenty-four hours. This meant leaving the log home he had put up and a crop about ready to harvest on the two acres of stump-land cleared. Mr. Collins having just sold everything he owned, had one hundred dollars in gold on him and easily bought Gorman out.

Collins worked hard and by the next fall had broken up fifteen more acres and planted them with corn and potatoes. Early purchases were a team of oxen and a cow. After the first meager harvest was in, Collins returned to Massachusetts for the rest of his family, who had traveled as far as Buffalo by rail, then on to their destination on the steamer Nominee, fastest boat on the river. It was captained by Russell Blakely, who proclaimed this achievement to every other vessel by fastening a new broom on the flag staff, as was the custom.

Upon reaching Saint Paul, it was the newly trimmed cupola on the Territorial Capitol Building that claimed the families' attention. The Nominee steamed up the river as far as Fort Snelling, their destination. A very steep hill led up to the fort, causing the Collins family to pull up their goods in small wagon loads.

Loren Collins, age twelve, had lifted, lugged, and climbed until he was about done in. Then his dad, after wrestling a white heifer to the top of the hill with a rope around her horns, handed Loren the rope, saying "Hold 'er while I get another load." The strain on his tired arms as the heifer bucked was almost too much. Then, Loren noticed the wagon. Tying his end of the rope around a wheel helped a lot and seemed a viable solution. About that time a dozen soldiers in all of their glory tooted their way out of the fort to take their turn at standing guard duty. The heifer gave a mighty lunge, the wagon became uncoupled in the center, and Loren found himself making a fast trip on his belly on the end of the rope, with the white heifer leading and a set of wagon wheels in the middle! The mishap caused great consternation among the representatives of Uncle Sam, bystanders, and Loren Collins, who never again reviewed the United States Army with the same amount of respect. The Collins family camped overnight, not reaching their destination on the west bank of the Mississippi River across from St. Anthony until the next day. Cattle were fed not far from where the Nicolette House stands.

When Logan Collins was older he took up a claim of his own. He worked it for six months. Then dark clouds filled with hail crowded in on a hot day to ruin everything he had worked for. The temperature dropped from almost one hundred degrees to somewhere in the sixties in less than an hour. Then it hit. Hail the size of hen's eggs propelled by a fifty-mile-per-hour wind shattered windows, went through his roof, and broke a cast iron stove. Logan crawled out from under a sturdy table into what he imagined a war zone might look like.

Everything loose had been blown away. Hail lay over a

foot deep on the east side of anything left standing. Logan surveyed his wrecked home, a sodden mess, and hobbled in his tight water-soaked boots toward Kenyon, three miles away. By the time he arrived he could hardly stand, yet couldn't get his boots off. It was plain to be seen that the storm had decimated every growing thing. There wasn't a pane of glass left in the little village, plus anyone who had not found shelter in time was wounded.

Logan had $1.50 in his pocket, which he showed to a landlord with a part of his hotel still half-dry. The man took pity on Logan's condition and let him stay without cost. Somehow, the cook scraped up a poor supper. Also at the table was Seagrave Smith, a Hastings lawyer. Smith urged Logan to give up trying to farm this poor land and become a lawyer, offering to teach him in his own firm.

Logan listened. Without ever going back to his demolished claim, he first became a lawyer under the tutelage of Smith, then went on to end his life at eighty-nine as Honorable Judge Logan W. Collins.

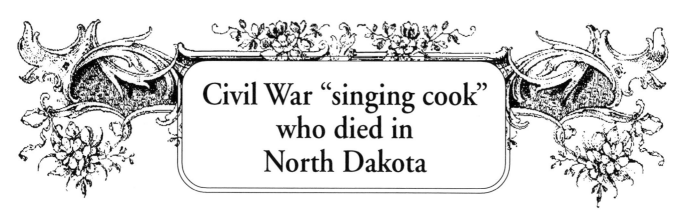

Civil War "singing cook" who died in North Dakota

"Old Shady", better known as Blakely Durant, was not only General Sherman's favorite cook but his most ardent admirer, his "singin' black cook", as he affectionately called him. Durant joined the Seventy-first Ohio Volunteer Infantry, the regiment that was General Sherman's division. From the very first, he was detailed as cook for the officers mess. He followed Sherman after Shiloh, seeing him constantly.

Old Shady became a well-known caterer for various groups of Union officers and their ladies. It was Sherman who named him that, with the hero of the famous march "From the Atlantic to the Sea" even making him the subject of an extended sketch in his "Memoirs of the War", published in 1888.

It was while doing a hitch on a gunboat at Milliken's Bend during the winter of 1863 that Old Shady and his battered guitar really gained the attention of generals. Although detailed to do the cooking, Old Shady found other ways to show his bravery and loyalty. At one point, when the regiment had to retreat in short order, they left their flag behind. Noticing this, Old Shady sneaked back into dangerous territory to retrieve it, delivering the colors in grand style. While he saved the flag, his old guitar became a casualty.

Soon after, the grateful soldiers replaced the guitar with a fine fancy one, which proved to be instrumental to Old Shady's composing the favorite Civil War song entitled "Old Shady". It went like this: 'Yah! Yah! Yah! Come laugh wid me, De white folks Old Shady am free, I spec' de year of Ju-be-lee am a-comin', Hail, mighty day.' There were six verses, each of which put the misery of his people to music.

Blakely Durant died in Grand Forks, North Dakota, on September 20, 1894, at the age of sixty-four. In his flattering account of Old Shady, as published in the North American Review, General Sherman wrote of this famous singing cook, "I do believe that since the prophet Jeremiah bade the Jews to sing for joy among the chiefs of the nations, because of their deliverance from the house of bondage, no truer song of gladness ever ascended from the lips of men than when Old Shady sang the pure melody of this song of deliverance from the bonds of slavery."

Old Shady made Grand Forks his home the last twenty years of his life. His son is a graduate of the North Dakota University.

Jane G. Swisshelm, woman with a fighting spirit!

A fiery, pro-slavery man from the South named General Sam Lowrie ran things in Stearns County from St. Cloud. He was not only a southern gentleman, but a Democrat. He was used to having the last word, king of whatever hill he chose to occupy. Until Jane Swisshelm came along, that is. The printed word was her weapon. She seemed always ready to attack anything that hobbled the rights of women. She was grim faced, an agitator, did not shy from using violent language.

Jane Grey Cannon, daughter of Irish Presbyterian parents, married James Swisshelm. At this time neither slaves or women had been emancipated and a belligerent Jane went to bat for women's rights. James was embarrassed by his rebel-wife, who wanted to get out and make speeches, to change the way women were required to dress, to write. But, alas, James was old fashioned as were his ideas. Jane abhorred the slavery system which she became more aware of during a visit to Kentucky. It didn't take long before Jane was helping Negroes head north via the "underground railroad". One of the first things she did after returning to St. Cloud was begin a series of attacks against slavery, contributed to a magazine published in Pittsburgh, called *The Spirit of Liberty*.

James ended the troubled marriage when he saw that he could not control his wife's next move, what she might do next. The business James was in was sinking fast and when he traded what remained of it for a panther to roam around the house, it was the end. No more. Jane could take no more. Even so, and as unhappy as he was, James still refused to grant her a divorce. She solved that problem by just leaving, going west.

Jane arrived on a stagecoach in St. Cloud where friendly relatives let her stay. As soon as she arrived, she began casting around for ways to support herself and her baby daughter. After a few days, she found work on a local paper. For her services, she was given St. Cloud town lots. It was near this time that General Lowrie, who owned a home on the Mississippi staffed by many of the slaves brought from a southern estate, drew her attention. Did he not know or care that Minnesota was free territory? Jane sent fiery missiles in print his way.

Thinking to soften her ferocity, General Lowrie tactfully approached the fact that perhaps Jane could better her lot by supporting President Buchanan, a Democrat. Instead of the expected explosion, Jane said she would do what she could to get Buchanan elected. A long article in the *St. Cloud Visitor* written by Jane was more like the Jane everyone knew. It was not only long, but written in a satirical way that slashed Buchanan to the bone!

Jane itemized point-by-point, what she saw wrong with the Buchanan platform, all of them uncomplimentary. The general became livid with anger and had his lawyer deliver a lecture that scathed Jane in every way possible. She reciprocated with an article that took from prominent women of St. Cloud their reputations. She wrote they sat up all night playing poker with men. Not long after, the office of *The Visitor* was vandalized, with much damage done. The press was not only broken, but dumped into the river. A note on the door stated: "If you ever again attempt to publish a paper in St. Cloud, you yourself will be summarily dealt with as your office has been." These were strong words! General Lowrie's henchmen were

suspected.

However, Jane was not without friends who came to her rescue. A public meeting was held to decide what should and could be done. Jane had her lawyer write up her will. She hired a sure shooter with an infallible eye to act as her bodyguard. There was, indeed, danger that she might fall into the hands of a mob. Her guard was prompted to shoot her through the head should this occur. At the meeting she accused Lowrie and several others of wrecking her office, ruining her presses. She spoke until the room was filled with men who threatened to shoot.

Thanks to public interest, enough money was raised to allow Mrs. Swisshelm to go back to publishing her paper. This happy resolution of a troublesome affair did not end there. Libel suits, along with other problems finally forced her to give up the project. Jane was down, but hardly defeated for she soon started another sheet called the unlikely name of *The Democrat*, exactly what she was not.

Jane had, in the opinion of the public, defeated the general and was left alone to print what she pleased without problems. She became a nurse in the Civil War. She lived in a tiny cabin in Swissvale, Pennsylvania, until she died. It has to be said that hers was, indeed, a colorful life!

Heroic pioneer women who fought back bravely

Our local history is peopled with the accomplishments of strong women – long before a woman could vote. Although you may have never heard her name, Guri Enderson had to be close to the top of our strong pioneer ladies. But her title – had there been one – would have just been "pioneer wife."

In 1862, Guri left a snug settlement in Norway to come to northern Minnesota to marry Lars Enderson. She promised to follow him anywhere, and she did. Her "anywhere" turned out to be a clearing in a timberland on the shores of a lake.

Indian uprisings were the norm during those days. The Indians had been double-crossed by white treaty makers too many times. Innocent settlers were paying the price.

Just as dark was settling one night, Indians complete with war paint swooped onto the Enderson land. Guri knew the Enderson men – Lars and their two sons – should be heading home from an afternoon of cutting wood.

To the accompaniment of warrior cries renting the quiet night, Guri clutched her baby daughter, putting her down only long enough to drag what furniture they had that wasn't nailed to the wall in front of the door. Where were her men?

Guri picked up the baby and peeped through a crack in a shutter just in time to see her Lars go down with an arrow in his back. Guri prayed for strength as the commotion gradually drew further away as night thickened.

Putting the baby down, Guri crept into the darkness outside. It was raining. Her sons had not come home yet. As Guri felt her way through the darkness, she berated herself for answering that request from America of the man who needed a wife! He turned out to be a fine man...but she didn't know about the Indians. In his letter

he had called them "heathens." Since there were no so-called heathens in Norway, she didn't know what he meant.

Then she stumbled on something. Running her hands over it, she recognized the body of her eldest son. The boys had not escaped. She dragged his body inside the cabin and returned to find Lars. She found him near the watering trough. He wasn't breathing. Too numb to cry, Guri searched for her two daughters. They had been picking berries. They did not answer her calls.

Finally, Guri gathered up her baby and with a last look at her beloved Lars and son, headed off into the wet darkness for the Oscar Erickson cabin twelve miles away. At dawn she found herself in a clearing she recognized. And she should have – it was her own. She had walked all night in a circle!

A wisp of smoke from their chimney attracted her attention. Did Indians make fires in a fireplace? She didn't think so.

Cautiously, Guri made her way to the shuttered window of their cabin and peeked in. There, the son she had dragged inside was trying to heat some water. He had only a shoulder wound. It was a joyful reunion.

The only things the Indians had left behind were a battered wagon and two half-broken steers they could not catch. One had an arrow in its rump. After a horrible, frantic struggle, Guri got the critters harnessed to the wagon. Again, with the boy creeping ahead to watch for Indians, she headed for the Erickson cabin.

The steers plunged off the trail first on one side and then the other. They got hung up on stumps and straddled trees. During the later part of the afternoon, they came to the Erickson cabin. It was strangely quiet. Mr. Erickson and another man had met Lars's fate.

What to do?

The boy urged, "C'mon, Ma, there is still Indians all over."

Guri answered, "First see if they're plumb dead."

The men had lost a lot of blood. One of them didn't seem exactly "plumb dead" to Guri, so they took him along.

"Help me hist 'em in the wagon," she said.

The boy's pain was worsening. They had to hurry. It was all Guri could do to head the ornery oxen toward the trail. The smell of blood spooks most animals.

The sun had just set when they pulled into a small military settlement. Men looked in wonder at the obstinate, exhausted beasts Guri had driven, marveling at her strength and determination.

Guri thought she was dreaming when her two girls came flying around a corner of the fort, pigtails flying. They had escaped when the marauders had gotten drunk and gone to sleep.

Another local pioneer lady won her battle in quite another way. It was said she was writing a letter to relatives back east with her back to the cabin door. A shadow fell over her paper and she turned to see an Indian in suspended animation, a club half-raised. He was peering over her shoulder at the funny marks she was making on the paper. He was captivated.

Taking advantage of the situation, the lady, who was an officer's wife, pointed to a chair and shoved the paper toward him. After a few minutes of making marks on the paper, he slipped out the door, taking the pencil and paper with him. What must have been ice water in her veins melted as soon as he had left and she fainted.

For each brave man there were at least two brave women – his mother and his wife.

It has always been thus.

The doctor who foisted fad diets on pioneers – over 100 years ago!

Dr. H.S. Tanner was no stranger to this part of the country. In the late 1880s as he made his way from community to community administering to the ill.

While he also dispensed pills, he had a solid theory which he had trouble selling to the general populace. He had doctored, so he said, in Minneapolis in 1880 and had no trouble curing many patients there with his idea.

Dr. Tanner contended, "The human stomach is nothing but a nuisance...good only to stir up aches and pains of all sorts of ailments on mankind."

To support this belief, he often quoted biblical saints who went on periods of fasting and came out the better for it.

Dr. Tanner was born in England and was far from being a good specimen of health, plagued as he was with asthma, rheumatism and heart trouble. The ten-day fasts he often took were not long enough to prove his point, he said, and one day set out to settle once and for all the value of his theory. He vowed not to let one morsel of any kind of food pass his lips for forty days!

Dr. Tanner chose a room in Clarendon Hall of the New York Medical College where the findings of his experiment could hardly be a cause of dispute. To make sure it wasn't a hoax, his clothing was examined thoroughly. A guard was posted outside his door to make sure no food was smuggled in.

Newspaper reporters jumped on the stunt and at first it made the front pages. As time passed, it receded into the background. However, by the time the third week arrived, and Dr. Tanner was still alive, stories of all kinds abounded. One paper claimed he had lockjaw. Others said he had lapsed into delirium and was hopelessly insane. Wagers were made as to how long he could hold out.

Doctors put in bids for his remains, to which Dr. Tan-

ner readily agreed – as long as they waited until he was done with them himself!

Naturally, since he had been the local medic in these parts, people here took special interest and wished news did not travel so slowly. As the end of the forty days neared, Dr. Tanner's weight dropped from 180 pounds to 130. He tried to send encouraging messages often to his friends in Minneapolis, but even so headlines read: "How Soon Will The End Come?"

He even received a number of marriage proposals.

Poetry was written in honor of the event. One poem went like this:

"Hurrah, hurrah, for Tanner true.
Hurrah for the stalwart stomach, too.
And when the glorious time draws near,
When meals consist of water clear,
And will have no boarding-house mistress to fear,
Be the stomach gold mounted and this engraved:
'Here lies the stomach that takes   the cake,
That never for custard pie has craved,
And has gone forty days without beef steak!"

When Dr. Tanner finally emerged, he had not only lost weight but was two inches shorter. He had done the same thing one other time, he claimed, but only Dr. A. Moyer of Minneapolis had known about it.

It is recalled that at the victorious end of the fast, Dr. Tanner was greeted by a New York demonstration that rivaled the one given Lindberg. Telephone books were torn up and thrown out the windows of high buildings. Whistles blew. Crowds gathered.

Dr. Tanner's first meal consisted of a small glass of milk and a hunk of watermelon. He moved to California, where he founded a diet sect that failed to catch on. Dr. Tanner died in San Diego in January 1919 at the age of 87.

"We ain't dirty — I believe in sanitary!"

A woman's cry to those who would drag her away

Lily climbed down the spokes of the wagon wheel after four brothers and two sisters. Pa took a good look around while he unhitched Dan and Dolly, announcing "Might as well stay here a spell. Horses need a rest. Looks like good broom-making country, too."

To the right of them, up a side hill, grew a stand of young poplar trees the right size for broom handles. On the left was a brown dry-lookin' swamp with tall wide-bladed grass higher than Lily's head, just right for the business end of the broom.

John, the oldest son, looked back at old Belle, pulling a rickety buggy that held Granny and Ma along with anything else that could hang on, be stacked or tied.

"Is that a town 'way yonder there?" Ma asked. "If it is, this's the spot we been searchin' for. Lookit all that broom grass! Tom, come help Granny down."

Having come from "no where" South Dakota to "where are we" Minnesota, they were all tired. Had been on the road, if you could call it that, almost a week. A soft tuft of broom grass with a quilt over it made a fair bed for granny, who was close to 90.

"You can relax, Granny. Ain't no poison snakes here," Tom yelled in her best ear. She coughed, nodded her thanks and promptly fell asleep.

Pa made a fire and took care of the horses while Ma 'scratched what was left of the grub together. It wasn't much. The girls disappeared into the tall grasses of the swamp while the boys headed for the poplar hill, hatchets in hand, to cut broom handles.

In a half-hour they'd eaten what there was. With Granny fed and bedded down for the night, everybody set to making brooms. Most people welcomed a new broom and making one took time and cut-up hands something terrible. In the morning some of the kids could go house to house (or shack to shack, more truthful) as Pa hit up the store keeper for a trade for things they just had to have. Pa was good at that.

Ma's brow was mostly wrinkles, though she'd just turned 40. Already they had spotted a shack they could all squeeze into for awhile. Pa promised they'd have a fine house come spring. Granny's cough was worse. Lily looked peaked, too. The first night in the shack Pa dug out his old fiddle and near scared the critters hiding in the corners and skitterin' along the roof poles to death in his effort to cheer everyone up with a hoe-down. Then, "Annie Laurie". It didn't help much.

Granny's cough was almost constant now. They hauled her to the local medic everybody swore by. Dr. Bean shook his head and asked, "How many live in your place?"

"Snoopy!" Ma hissed under her breath.

Pa shuffled and said, "Ten, with granny. We made bunks wide enough for two all around the walls. Real comfy. Gonna build a fine house in the spring, my four boys and me are."

Doctor Bean looked straight at Pa, saying, "You have to get your mother into a sanitarium. There's one in the next town. Right away!"

"Well, we ain't dirty! I believe in sanitary!" Ma blazed.

"I'm sure you do," doc said, patting her arm. "But tuberculosis is sweeping the country. Spreads like wildfire. The rest of your family has to be tested. In the morning. I'll take Granny on over right now."

On the way back home Ma's eyes looked worried. Real worried. If she was to be hells-fire honest, she'd have to admit she'd heard almost everybody cough now and then. Her, too. She'd never been so weary. Pa was losin' weight. All his fast fiddlin' wasn't foolin' her. Not one bit, it didn't.

During the remaining months of the winter and spring, one by one, they joined those in the sanitarium. Soon after she'd arrived, Granny made the first trip in their family to the graveyard.

The procedure for doctoring the disease seemed to be putting everybody to bed out on sun-porches and opening the windows wide. The sun shone mighty scant, it seemed to Ma. They were given woolen caps to wear. Hefty big jugs, called "pigs", was filled with hot water, wrapped in layers of newspaper, and put in bed with them to help keep them warm. Pa said they was even. The first half of the night the jugs kept them warm and the last half they kept the jugs warm.

As the dark months dragged on, a few weeks apart the entire family joined Granny until only Ma and Lily were left. Lily was a puzzlement. She'd come in white as death, skin over bones and got neither better nor worse. Not even Doc Bean could explain it. Ma was so sick herself she didn't know when Pa's turn came. That left "little Lily" as the nurses had taken to calling her. At last spring came and the sun gained strength. Lily seemed to gain along with it. She'd quit coughing. With nowhere else to go, Dr. Bean took her along home with him.

Eighty-five years later, on April 13, Lily was given a party by the people in her church where she'd taught many a class. She was always thin, but her brown eyes were bright and happy. It was here she told the story of the brooms and the sad winter that followed.

"They was always extra good to me. I was always puny and tired. Never could do my share of the work. I should have gone before those big strong brothers and sisters, wouldn't you think?

"Don't seem much use to try and figure out life, does it?"

No one disagreed.

Vanished local towns you've never heard of!

A hundred years ago the countryside was peppered with small towns that have now left without a trace. Where'd they go? Several that come to mind are Topelius, Linnell and Mallard.

Topelius was the smallest of the trio. In fact, they didn't get much smaller. It was located several miles east of Bluffton, south of the railroad tracks. One old timer remembers it already being an old beat-up town in 1915 when he was a kid in Bluffton. Another recalls a faded sign over a dusty road that read: Topelius.

A fellow who worked on the railroad still recalls how hard the crew worked when nearing Topelius. They served the coldest beer around. Many agree there was a fairly busy depot there. It joined history so effortlessly that no one can come close to putting a date on just when the Topelius sign came down.

I.E. (Charlie) Linnell, one of my ancestors, moved from Iowa to a homestead in Becker County, a mile east of where Ponsford stands today. That first winter of 1880 was memorable. Snow measured four feet on the level, making it impossible for settlers to travel more than a mile or two. That is when Charlie knew he had to start a trading post. He started one in his home in 1881. He had room to only stock necessities and gathered furs and pelts from the settlers and Indians.

In 1882, his home also became the site of a post office. The town was named for Abigail Linnell, a widow who homesteaded where Ponsford now stands. She was commissioned Becker County's first postmistress in 1883. She was Charlie's mother. Charlie and Abigail kept the post office going – also on Abigail's land – until Ponsford took over. Then she and Charlie moved far west where homesteading was easier, the winters shorter and a dollar didn't

look so big. Abigail lived to be nearly one hundred years old.

Despite the fact that Mallard was quite a metropolis compared to many neighboring towns, with a population of 400 souls, it, too, bit the dust in 1939.

Mallard consisted of sixteen city blocks divided into twelve lots. Its avenues were named Itaska, Robinson, Roma, Sinker and University, with its main thoroughfare called Sibley Avenue. Many who worked on the new railroad being built lived there (they received twelve cents per hour of hard work), as well as many loggers, who took advantage of living in town.

Harry Sinker's place, The Pioneer Store, carried $40,000 worth of merchandise. It served everyone who could find a way of getting to it. Other businesses besides Sinker's were another general store, drug store, livery stable, hotel, school, restaurant, barber shop, dance hall, five saloons, post office and a newspaper called *The Mallard Call*. The first building went up in Mallard in 1901, giving it a life span of only thirty-eight years.

However, in that short time, it made enough of an impression for an unknown poet to write an untitled poem that could well be the cry of every small place that returned to dust:

Mallard lost its grip and years later on,
The town was here but the buildings were gone.
From much strife and oppositions, everywhere found,
And the buildings were leveled to the ground.
Absence of friends and few to stand guard,
It suffered long and died very hard.

"Gee! Haw!"

Herbert & Otto Sellnow
Oxen delivered many pioneer families safely to the new frontier.

Without the slow, sometimes stubborn and always aggravating ox, fewer pioneers would have safely reached their destinations.

Probably no expedition proved this more than a small group of Norwegian immigrants preparing to head for a territory called "Dakota".

John Knutson bought two, huge oxen, offered for sale near Austin, Minnesota, for the trip. The critters cost Knutson $100 – probably the best money he ever spent. Huge as they were, the two oxen were gentle and obedient.

On May 15, 1873, Knutson and his team of oxen, along with twelve other covered wagons and several prairie schooners, began what was to be a two-month trek over several hundred dusty miles.

Almost immediately, Knutson's huge critters were put to the test. The caravan came to a creek that had overflowed its banks. It was deep, with a swift current. Only Knutson's monsters could walk on the bottom, heads held high. The other oxen and horses floundered, upsetting the first few wagons. Finally, enough log chains were hooked together to reach across the stream. Knutson's pow-

erful brutes pulled the wagons, one by one, to the safety of dry land.

Once the wagons were safely across, two little boys, Cornelius Troovien and Peder Knutson, were ordered to drive the cattle across the flooded creek. Cornelius was lucky enough to clamber aboard the back of the last cow into the water. Scared spitless, Peder wondered how he was going to cross.

Just as Peder was about to yell for help, a stray ox entered the water. Grabbing its tail, Peder hung on for all he was worth. It swam faster and faster, breezing past the herd of cows, where Cornelius was desperately trying to keep his seat on the cow's slippery back.

Another frightening incident occurred just after the caravan had crossed a railroad track. A train thundering by panicked the two young teams of oxen, hitched one ahead of the other to Ole Troovien's wagon. They left the trail, and swung off across a slough. Behind them bumped the wagon, nearly overturning.

Terrified, Mrs. Troovien sat on the wagon floor, clutching baby Kristi with one hand, while hanging on to a heavy chest for dear life with the other. Left behind, scared out of his wits, Ole stood yelling, "Haw! Haw!", with no effect on the runaways.

Beyond the slough, the team ran astraddle a tamarack tree, stopped, then calmly began to graze. It was a pale and trembling young woman with screaming baby who climbed down from the wagon to wait for Ole.

Despite swollen streams and runaway wagons, the immigrants reached Dakota Territory on July 14, 1873 – grateful to Knutson's team of oxen.

Author's note: This vignette was taken from the book, *The Immigrants' Trek*, by Gustav O. Sandro, sent in by Emma Kirkwald, Retirement Home, Hendricks, Minnesota.

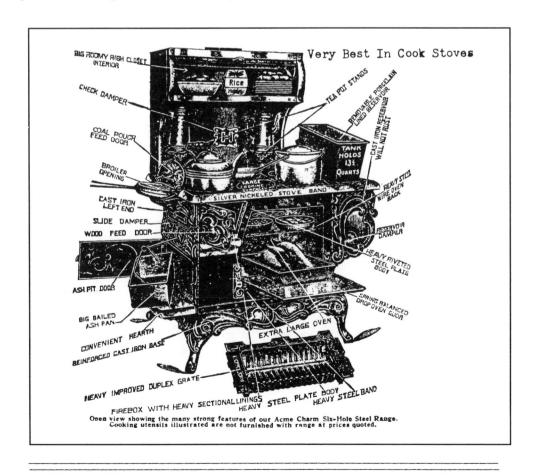

Open view showing the many strong features of our Acme Charm Six-Hole Steel Range. Cooking utensils illustrated are not furnished with range at prices quoted.

Vicious horns of Minnesota's "Beelzebub the Bull" terrified screaming crowds!

Inspiration struck William G. LeDuc with such force that the paper he was reading slipped from his hands. There was to be a World's Fair in the Crystal Palace in New York.

"How fine it would be, in this year of 1853," he mused "if the territory of Minnesota could be represented in so grand a structure, filled with exhibits from all over the world!"

LeDuc then set about persuading Governor Alexander Ramsey to sponsor a bill in the territorial legislature, that would authorize $300 for a Minnesota exhibit. The bill passed, with LeDuc delegated to spend the money to best advantage.

M. Cunradie, trading post owner on the Upper Mississippi, who claimed to be a foster brother of Louis Napoleon, appointed himself to "help" LeDuc find a "suitable" exhibit. What Cunradie thought suitable was one of the biggest buffalo bulls LeDuc had ever seen.

"You see?" pressed Cunradie. "The peeples see zis fine bool and says to heemself, 'Meenisota? Vare iss dat? I mus' go der!'." The price was $300 and LeDuc, most impressed, bought the bull.

Getting the bull into a boxcar for the train ride to St. Paul was an experience LeDuc tried to forget. Once in St. Paul, the bull had to be "walked" to the wharf, where the Steamer Ben Franklin awaited its passengers. Again, the animal, not being used to so many people, made a laughingstock out of LeDuc. It took another heroic struggle to get the bull, now known as "Beelzebub", aboard the Ben Franklin.

Upon arrival in St. Louis, where LeDuc and his prize Minnesota Territory exhibit had to transfer to another steamer, Beelzebub declined to use the runway when he left the boat. Instead, he jumped overboard, scrambled up the muddy riverbank, and, head swinging, went on a rampage down a main city street. Hogsheads of sugar, cotton bales and crates of squawking chickens flew off his vicious horns.

On a side trip down a fancy residential street, Beelzebub reduced impeccably dressed ladies to screams. Otherwise sedate teams of fine horses flew from his advance in terror.

LeDuc, beside himself with anguish, finally rounded up Beelzebub and got him on board the Cincinnati-bound steamer. By this time, LeDuc, tired of promoting Minnesota Territory, had lost his enthusiasm for Cunradie's bull.

In Cincinnati, LeDuc tried to sell his "prize specimen of bison" to a butcher. The butcher hung up on him. Next, he tried to sell the critter to a side-show owner – cheap. That fell through, too.

Then, it was time to wrestle the bull into a cattle car for the last leg of the World's Fair trip.

Arriving in New York City on Sunday, LeDuc could find no official to whom he could deliver Beelzebub. With help, he managed to get the bull off the train and to a livery stable.

Next day, believing his troubles were over, LeDuc contacted the fair official in charge of exhibits. To his dismay, the official refused the Minnesota exhibit! There was no place to "confine such a behemoth critter," the official explained.

Discouraged and broke, LeDuc appealed to journalist

Horace Greeley, who could offer no solution. In desperation, LeDuc wrote to Cunradie for assistance. He replied: "My dear fren, I haf ze poignant regret. I tok wat some leetle money I haf an' haf one tremendous spree wen I hear zat my bison haf reach New York."

Actually sick now with worry, LeDuc tried to sell the buffalo to P.T. Barnum, who said he was not in the market for that kind of freak. Cost of transportation prohibited giving the animal to Louis Napoleon, as a gift from the territory of Minnesota.

At last, to LeDuc's immense relief, the manager of a carnival bought Beelzebub for $300, payable in installments that remain unpaid today.

HOW ST. PAUL FEELS ABOUT IT.

Resolved, By the Chamber of Commerce of the city of St. Paul, representing its citizens in every department of business and activity, that we earnestly protest against the issuance of an order for a recount of this city.--From resolutions adopted by the St. Paul Chamber of Commerce.

IT MEANS WAR

The Mask of Hypocrisy Torn from the Malignant Face of St. Paul.

A Dastardly Outrage Committed on Minneapolis Citizens by the St. Paul Gang.

The Plunderers Carry off a Vast Quantity of Local Census Material.

A Wave of Indignation Sweeps Over the City---A Meeting Called.

Cartoon and Headline from in Twin City Newspapers at the time of the St. Paul-Minneapolis Census Fight
(Minneapolis Journal - June 18, 1890 and July 21, 1890)

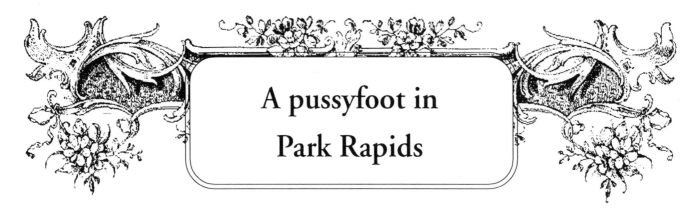

A pussyfoot in Park Rapids

Pussyfoot took it upon himself to clear the country, maybe even the world, of all the booze. The year was 1906, before prohibition.

Pussyfoot's real name was W.E. Johnson, a representative of the Anti-Saloon League. He acquired the name "Pussyfoot" in Oklahoma after a fight with a pool room proprietor suspected of selling liquor.

Pussyfoot disguised himself as a drunken cattleman, then went to the pool hall to buy a drink. When offered sarsaparilla instead, he put up such a fuss the proprietor gave in and produced the real thing.

Aha! Pussyfoot had the proprietor. He immediately overpowered and arrested him.

An Oklahoma newspaper called Johnson "a booze-bustin' old pussyfoot." The name stuck and followed him wherever he went.

While trying to dry up the British Isles before the Oklahoma incident, he lost an eye. Soon after Pussyfoot learned to cope with just one eye, he learned about the many problems booze was causing for the Indians in northwestern Minnesota and made up his mind to do something about it.

The Indians had recently been granted the right to dispose of their timber and lands as they saw fit. Once money was in their hands, it was soon exchanged for booze...and it took very little rum to make an Indian drunk! Saloons flourished. It was recorded that there was one saloon for every one hundred Indians. Park Rapids saloon owners were becoming rich doing a landslide business. Had they known that disaster lay just around the corner, it would have wiped the smiles off their faces, even all the way to the bank!

Defrauding drunk Indians of everything they owned had become an all too popular business for too many people. To combat the problem, government representatives decided to enforce the old Indian Treaty of 1855 which made selling liquor to Indians a serious federal offense.

Theodore Roosevelt heard about Pussyfoot, admired his daring exploits, and appointed him a "Special Officer" to enforce anti-liquor laws in Indian Territories and Reservations. He sent Pussyfoot to the White Earth Reservation. Most trade centered around Cass Lake, Walker and

Bemidji. Naturally, law officers struck there first. Cass Lake and Walker were allowed to keep two saloons each.

The Indians were furious. They funneled their business toward Park Rapids, which swiftly became a mecca for all kinds of crime. A letter of protest was rushed to Washington via the *Park Rapids Enterprise* and the *Hubbard County Clipper.* Then Pussyfoot struck.

Park Rapids was never the same. At the time, sixty grog dealers were in business. Pussyfoot gave them ten days to remove stock from their back rooms and bottles from their shelves. Saloon keepers threatened to fight. They signed petitions, pulled strings and called meetings, all to no avail.

On the eleventh day after the warning from Pussyfoot, everything started quietly enough with business as usual. Also, as usual, the noon train pulled into the station. It was definitely most unusual, however, when a horde of lawmen poured from the cars! Pussyfoot let the brigade toward the nearest saloon.

Once action started, proprietors were pushed into corners. Shelves were ripped down. Glass and bottles were shattered. Some establishments were simply burned to the ground. In others, any bottles not already broken were carried to the middle of the street in cases and set up in rows for target practice. Muddy ruts soon ran with booze.

Pussyfoot did not let his efforts stop with Park Rapids. He wrote books entitled "The Liquor Problem in Russia" and "The Federal Government and the Liquor Traffic." Both could be had for $1.00 each. He traveled extensively and was a popular speaker.

Wherever Pussyfoot traveled, it was agreed by home-loving townspeople that he and his cohorts had made Park Rapids once again a safe place in which to raise a family. Pussyfoot's plans had, in this case at least, proved effective.

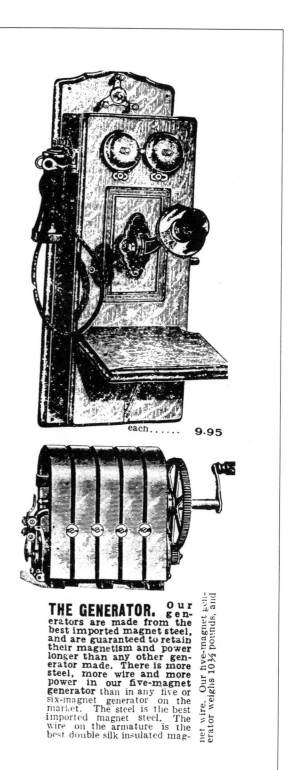

each...... 9.95

THE GENERATOR. Our generators are made from the best imported magnet steel, and are guaranteed to retain their magnetism and power longer than any other generator made. There is more steel, more wire and more power in our five-magnet generator than in any five or six-magnet generator on the market. The steel is the best imported magnet steel. The wire on the armature is the best double silk insulated magnet wire. Our five-magnet generator weighs 10½ pounds, and

Circuit riders

As a young man, frontier clergyman Frances Asbury received this advice from his teacher: "Son, from now on your back must learn to fit any man's bed." He could have added, "or no bed at all," since circuit riders spent many nights rolled up in a blanket on a hearth.

Early circuit riders were unpretentious men clothed in plain dark garments that invariably showed wear and tear. They often appeared a bit odd or peculiar to others.

The name, circuit rider, was given them because they had no special charge; the whole frontier was their parish. The pop tune "CC Rider" also was inspired by these men. Many married Indian women – they needed a woman at home who was tough enough to meet the challenges of the frontier. And, since many pioneer men had Indian wives, the marriage often helped the clergyman relate to his "congregation".

Frances Asbury, John Nevin, J.H. Helmuths, Philip Otterbein, Archbishop John Ireland and dozens of others endured whatever hardships plagued the pioneers. They put aside personal comfort to ride sad-looking horses from dugout to dugout, cabin to cabin, summer and winter. They knew how eagerly they were awaited and how sorely they were needed for morals as well as morale.

In addition to preaching, marrying, burying and baptizing, clergymen were expected to lend a hand with the work wherever they stayed. Pastor Norelious, Red Wing, had to pitch in and help Gustave Edistrom and his neighbors sod the barn roof before he could get to preaching.

Often, an ox team seemed an indispensable tool for effective preaching, as it pulled the all-important Sunday School Wagon. The wagon was loaded with Bibles and other religious literature, usually the only printed word available. Pioneer children learned to read, and learned the Bible, all in one operation.

With the exception of a few dozen, most circuit riders substituted zeal for school. Being able to read the Bible was all the training that was necessary. Anybody with the inclination to preach, who could also shout, threaten, cajole and sometimes pound the pulpit for emphasis, made a name for himself.

Once, when Rev. Henderson of Hutchinson, was pummeling a hastily-built pulpit, it collapsed under his ministrations, destroying the atmosphere of doom it had taken him two hours to create. Much to Henderson's consternation, his audience broke into gales of laughter and scattered until the next meeting was called.

A circuit rider was respected, whatever the faith, but they came in for their share of ribbing, too: Mr. Secomb, father of Methodism in Minneapolis, was going to St. Paul to preach in 1849. His transportation was a dugout and his companion, Mr. Draper.

Below the falls, their dugout tipped, dumping them into the river. They were so sodden that St. Paul had to get along without them that day. It was considered a great joke, and for months the preacher was asked "if he was converted to immersion...now that he practiced it."

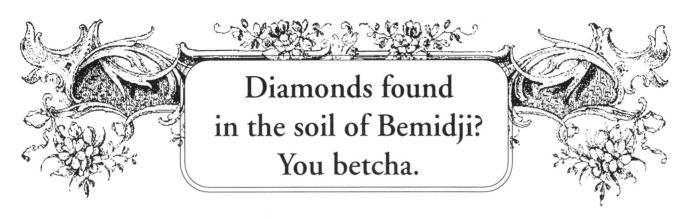

Diamonds found in the soil of Bemidji? You betcha.

The place was the Bemidji State College football stadium on an unseasonably sweltering afternoon, May 22, 1965. The event, our second son's graduation from college. Conditions? Crowded! Beyond the speaker on a portable stage who was valiantly struggling to cut his address in half lay Lake Bemidji. Sparkling, Inviting.

The young lady beside me who was to become my daughter-in-law in a few months sat proudly, eyes riveted on the same figure sporting mortarboard and gown whom Dad and I had come to see. I glanced at the glittering diamond on her finger, still so new she could count the times it had been put in water.

Then away went my thoughts like the Haley's Comet, back in time to almost a full century ago. I no longer noticed the heat. The unrelenting bleacher-seat. The speech could have been in Swahile. Besides, the sound system left much to be desired so I turned to my own thoughts.

For me, it was 1894. A homesteader, whose name has sifted away with the sands of time, left his tiny cabin in a nearby clearing to walk on the shores of a lake called "a-place-a-river-runs-into-and-out-of-again" by his Chippewa neighbors. He idly kicked at rocks here and there.

The pioneer stopped short. The last rock he kicked split in half to reveal a brilliant interior. A black diamond! He'd never heard of one, but he knew some diamonds were more rare than others. Could this be one of them? He fell to his knees. Crawling now, he scrambled around, gathering more rocks that resembled it. When broken they all sparkled! This could be a real find! It was located so far north not many people had spent much time up here. Well, he wasn't going to be stupid. He would have to have them assayed in St. Paul.

Quickly filling his hat with the rocks, he hurried back to his cabin. Mum. He had to keep mum, he cautioned himself. He had to get to St. Paul where a pecunious friend by the name of Tami Bixby lived. He would know what to do.

During the week it took him to go from Bemidji to St. Paul via foot and canoe, the homesteader could think of nothing but his "find". It rivaled anything he had ever heard or read about, including the black diamonds of Africa. Mites, mosquitoes, and wood ticks went unnoticed while he dreamed.

Tami Bixby also became captivated by the black diamonds and alerted several other well-heeled friends. When a local firm who assayed the rock declared them to be, indeed, the real McCoy, they were sent to New York for final evaluation. The homesteader was ordered back to Bemidji with a satchel full of money and directions to buy up all the land he could lay hands on, with thirty-day options.

As the final date of the options closed in, Bixby and friends became edgy. What was taking so long? Then, the long awaited letter arrived...only to inform them the rocks were quartzite. Worthless. One of Nature's hoaxes.

However, the depressing news hardly dampened the enthusiastic ambitions of the group. They had seen the great sparkling lake. Walked beneath those magnificent pines. They proceeded to buy all of the land options and the "Bemidji Townsite Company" was formed.

A railroad was run in from Walker. Pamphlets extolling the many virtues of a town to be called Bemidji were distributed all the way to the Atlantic Seaboard. The area was a winner and within the year, Bixby's company realized $300,000 as a result of the homesteader's discovery.

Two elbows, one from each side, jabbed simultaneously into my middle to bring me back from wherever wandering minds go. A tall young man in the back row stood up and was at last less than a minute away from acquiring that coveted diploma.

While expectations for the "Black Diamonds of Bemidji" fell flat, I am happy to say the real one my son bought didn't. Today, more than a quarter of a century

after he put it on his girl's finger, it is more brilliant than ever!

Besides a good job, a home they built fifteen years ago, and two strapping fine sons, one of them in his first year of college, they are content and happy.

Yet, who can say the homesteader's dream was for naught? Bemidji is truly a gem of a town! Our "Star of the North."

North Dakota mayhem: Crooked Legs, Charlo, and Chaos!

Wherever Crooked Legs and Charlo appeared, chaos was soon to follow. They were invincible, feared far and wide. Both were formidable hunters. A few drams of rum and they turned into butchers, with their own families sometimes their victims. They celebrated everything with a "treat", like the time they killed as many beavers as they could manage to get home. It was on a day like that when Crooked Legs nearly killed his young wife by breaking her bones, stabbing her, while in a drunken frenzy.

Charlo's career as a fearless hunter was more brief but every bit as colorful. For a dram of rum, he sold his twelve-year-old daughter. An expedition in need of a hunter to keep them supplied with meat invited Charlo to go with them but he was afraid of the Sioux. However, a promise of a keg of rum changed his mind and he agreed to risk his life by going as far as Grand Forks.

Charlo flatly refused to go to Goose River where the Sioux held sway. Another "treat" and Charlo was ready to go at once and invade Sioux territory all by himself until he had to be restrained. Upon returning to his hogan he beat his wife to death, then begged for more rum to wash away the sorrow. Soon after Charlo became gravely ill. A medicine man was called but no amount of dancing, whooping, and pounding on a drum helped and Charlo died.

The wife of Crooked Legs had better luck. She survived and went with him to court when he was apprehended for all of the atrocities in his wake. During the demonstration Crooked Legs sealed himself in his tent, singing sad songs, proclaiming that he was not afraid to die. To his credit, when Judge Henry forgave him for all of his inhumane attacks because he was drunk, Crooked Legs sobered up.

Now that he was no longer drunk and knew what was going on and what terrible things he had done, his wife beat him senseless, then set him on fire!

Transient farm labors waiting for transportation at Casselton. Reproduction from Harper's Weekly, 1890.

Bismarck escapade ends with whiskey-soaked death!

Mike Fink, or "Mickie Phinck", as he signed his name, was the best dead-eye sharp shooter up and down the entire Red River Valley, so famous he was banned from entering any of the turkey-shoots. If Mike's name was on the docket, no-one else signed up.

The only thing that equaled Mike's prowess with a gun was the hardness of his heart. He failed to consider what pain or hurt he might be foisting on someone else just to pull one of his pranks. One of the atrocities he committed without a second thought was shooting the heel off a Negro...because he thought it would look better after such an operation. Courts on both sides of the river became familiar with his name.

Mike's two best friends were two harum-scarums named Carpenter and Talbot. They were very nearly as good with a gun as Mike. In fact, so sure of themselves, they often entertained a crowd by shooting a glass of whiskey from each other's head.

Then, one day they quarreled. However, in due time they announced their reconciliation. It was Fink who suggested, as evidence of their restored confidence in each other, that the three friends prove it by their old practice of shooting a glass of whiskey from the head of one of the others. The first shot fell to Mike. Carpenter took his place without flinching...but, not without fear as he knew the man.

As Carpenter fell, shot clean through the middle of his forehead, Fink remarked "Hey, Carpenter, you've spilled the whiskey!" He then deliberately blew smoke out of his rifle barrel. Feeling also compelled to say something, he cursed the spilled whiskey, cursed his rifle, cursed himself.

Later, while boasting that he had killed Carpenter on purpose, Talbot could stand no more and killed Fink on the spot. Talbot came to a bad end by drowning a few years later.

After this escapade, violence committees organized in each territory in an effort to wipe out these lawless, lascivious characters infesting the regions. The early courts, like the one in Bismarck, North Dakota, who dealt with this one, convicted many who were sent to penitentiaries.

Main Street, Bismarck, 1872-73. The place was then called Edminton

Sam

Sam waited impatiently for the 1975 Senior Citizen's Day Parade to start in Mitchell, South Dakota. For him, the parade was the pinnacle of a lifetime.

Sam was 91. Beneath him pranced the horse of his dreams – a gleaming gaited Tennessee Walker that could also dance. It had been purchased in Scotland for $500 from Ed Pillar. Sam gave the glistening neck a pat and smiled.

Sam was born S.W. Harbert on August 30, 1882, in a stone house nine miles south of Mitchell in Hanson County. His father, a latheman, was W.B. Harbert, married to Anna Fitzgerald of Chicago-Irish parentage. She weighed less than 100 pounds. When Sam was born, he was three days old before either his father or a doctor saw him.

Childhood was fraught with dangers, yet only one really petrified him. It was a fearsome critter his uncle called "Red-headed Rawbones", who lay in wait to gobble little boys who ventured too far into the waist-high grass, called red-top, that surrounded the cabin.

Rawbones scared Sam even more than the oxen did, when they ran away and he had to jump for his life. He was four. Rawbones was more terrible than the night the big rattle-snake crawled up the screen door while he was eating sup-per; more frightening than the time the house and barn burned down!

Sam's career as a rider began at the age of four, when he drove an ox while his father guided the plow. He became a professional bronc buster at seventeen.

An education of sorts was acquired by attending schools at Burton, often reached by using barrel-stave skis. The last formal schooling Sam had was a year at Dakota Wesleyan Preparatory School. Then, he returned to the life he loved – breaking horses.

Sam acquired his own first horse when he was nine. The first time he took his dad's team out he turned too short, tipping the drag on top of them. While working at the Gibson ranch, he rode a mule that sedately walked to the farther side of the pasture, threw him and trotted back home.

At eighteen, Sam was known as a top-notch hand at breaking horses. Horses that were "green broke" brought good prices in Iowa. This meant riding them one time. Sam got a dollar for each bronc he rode until it quit bucking. He worked fourteen-hour days, often breaking twenty broncs a day, all without the use of spurs since he loved and under-stood horses. It was dangerous, hot and dirty work that he never tired of.

In 1904, he married Susan, the first girl born in Hanson County. For courting, he drove a fine horse with a fancy buggy. He made extra money working as an auctioneer and square-dance caller. Susan died in 1964. Her greatest pride, next to her family, was owning the county's only piano when she was ten years old.

In 1913, Sam purchased 1,000 acres where he broke horses. Prices dropped and he lost everything. He and Su-san moved to Mitchell, where Sam ran the dray.

The next years included many moves, jobs and enter-prises. In 1951, Sam retired. He built a trailer court, and at the age of 83, married Nadine.

The last ten years of his life, Sam turned his entire atten-tion back to horses.

He rode in rodeos and parades. He was presented with a trophy for being the oldest rider in the Mitchell Stampede.

His greatest thrill came at the Huron State Fair, where before a filled grandstand he made his horse rear and waved his hat. The crowd loved it and he got a standing ovation.

It was his last triumph.

Several hospitalizations came in 1974 and 1975, from which he was lured by the reminder of an Appaloosa colt that needed training.

Two weeks later, on July 4, 1975, death claimed this stal-wart old bronc buster, just two weeks before his 93rd birth-day.

Author's note: This is condensed from the account, en-titled "Sam", written by Virgil Harbert, Mitchell, South Dakota, in tribute to his father.

Horrible accident of the high climber!

"D'you ever look into the eyes of a strappin' young fella, just you and him 'way up on the skeleton of a high-dock, with both of ya knowin' in less than two minutes he'd be dead?" Ben's boney shoulders shook with sobs, as if it happened yesterday. There was no way to comfort him; the image was still so clear.

Ben was one of the minority of people who was not bothered by heights. He was lightly built yet strong and sure-footed. He was among the "high climbers" who worked above the third floor. He had worked on a dozen or more of the early sky scrapers in New York City. Why? It was good pay. There was a depression on. Jobs were scarce...and, he had a family.

The terrible accident Ben couldn't forget happened while working on the high docks at Lake Superior in the early 1900s.

It was a climber's nightmare. Sun sparkling on water blinded them and hurt their eyes. Water, always moving, always restless, made them dizzy. A wind of more than four or five miles per hour was worst of all. It could throw a man off balance. Folks on the ground never gave things like this a thought.

Ben shoved a big red handkerchief into his striped over-all back pocket. "It was then, just like now. Money, money, money!. That's all our big boss cared about. We never even seen him. Well, I guess it's better now, there's safety laws they have to abide. I guess some inspectors keep an eye out.

"Back in those times, they figured to lose at least a man a week. Lose a man; hire another'n the next day. Still makes me sick. No climbers' boots, safety belts or good scaffolding. Tools didn't have to be on a line; let a hammer get knocked off an' a worker two floors below got it on the head. You slipped...you died! Well, not allus. I was lucky three times. Never heard of a safety line on our belt.

"I got blowed off a girder once, four stories up. Landed in a pile of sand a truck had just dumped for the cement crew. Jarred me up good an' scared th'hell outta me, but I didn't break no bones. That was a Poughkeepsie, New York.

"Another time I slipped off a brace so high up we was in the clouds. My foot slipped on a damp piece and suddenly I was airborne!" Ben smiled. "But, I was a quick one! Kept my weight down. A big pulley cable swung by an' I grabbed on for dear life. Pulled my shoulder out but I'd wrapped my legs around it, too, so I made it. Good thing I was so high up or I wouldn't have had time for that. Lots of fellas fell right inside the skeleton. They usually hit braces or girders on the way down an' broke their backs. Or their necks.

"The next time I fell...was the last. I'd just got a good start goin' up when I stepped on a loose bolt that rolled. It shouldn'ta been left there. Landed on my feet but both arches was broke. I figured my luck had run out. I'd saved my money an' had a good thrifty wife, bless her. Family was on their own. People who look at those early buildings don't know all that went into 'em!"

Ben walked to a window, gnarled hands behind him. "Wisht I could forget that young fella. His feet had slipped off a brace, but he'd caught on with one hand an' reached the other'n out to me. I was about six feet or so away. I wrapped my legs around that old streamer an' stretched for all I was worth. Stretched 'till it hurt. Hang tight, son! Hang on...you can make 'er. Just a little more! I yelled, but we both knew his hold was slippin'. He was heavier than I was. He stretched...an' I stretched an' prayed, but the tips of our fingers was still just inches apart. If I'd only had a rope or a hammer handle or anything...I could

maybe saved him.

"Just before he hit thin air he whispered, 'Tell'er how much I love 'er an' be careful.' Then...there was just me an' that empty streamer. I cried like a baby. I knowed he meant that young wife that was about ready to have his baby. Tellin' that little woman was the hardest thing this life has asked me to do in 90 years!"

The red handkerchief came out again.

Turning, he gave me a wobbly smile. "Well, gotta keep goin'. Guess I'll walk uptown." He settled a hat with an old-fashioned wide brim on his head at a bit of a rakish angle, the only clue left of the young dare-devil of yore who had made a good living in hard times by defying fate each day...and won!

As he went past I gave him a fierce hug, as much to settle my nerves as to show him appreciation of all his generation had done that to this day...goes unsung.

Alex was an interviewer's delight; the kind we dream about but seldom find. He began on the right end of the story without a nudge.

"I was born on the shore of Spirit Lake at the edge of Menagha on December 14, 1906. I started out with nine brothers and four sisters. Father's name was 'John' and mother was 'Anna'. Both came from Finland to this country when they were children. My folks settled in New York Mills several years before there was either a 'Sebeka' or a 'Menagha'. From New York Mills father moved his family to a location where Menagha now stands. It could only be reached by a thirty-mile deer trail. There was a mill and father went to work in it. By the time we were school age, a school had been built. Students could go as far as the eighth grade, but most didn't. There were a few little stores, too.

"Father bought two-hundred acres, mostly timber. He let us children go as far as the fourth grade, until we could read a bit and do a few sums. I really felt sick when school started the next year and I could not go. I knew learning was easy for me. But, I guess, father needed us to help clear land. We six oldest boys finally got one hundred acres ready for the plow.

"Clearing land is rough work. Then one day father bought a funny-looking machine called a 'stump puller'. It was drawn by our horses, 'Prince' and 'Nancy'. Father knew just where to put the chain on each stump. Some of them were big fellows. The team pulled until their bellies were almost on the ground. With a crack, those big stumps had to finally give up. You should have seen the dirt fly when they broke free! I'd give anything to see it again right now.

"For sports, we boys played on the Menagha Bluebirds

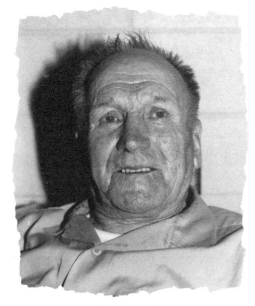

Alex Samuelson

Baseball Team at one time or another. Among ourselves, too. We rode horses and played winter games. There were so many of us!

"I'll never forget my ninth birthday. I could hardly believe my eyes when father hitched the stump puller to our house and yanked it down the road one-eighth of a mile to a spot he liked better. He pulled the barn over next. It put us kids in stitches to see our house and barn go down the road. Thinking back, I know he must have planned on it and built them on skids."

Alex stood up, stretched, and leaned against a tree near my chair. Then, "Say, you shoulda seen the crops that new land grew! We milked thirteen cows. We enjoyed the Indians. We trolloped back and forth along Leech Lake with our Chippewan friends. We learned to talk it fairly well. Whee! Did we have fun!"

"Did the Indians treat you like one of them?" I asked.

"I've heard they didn't make close friends with a lot of white people."

"Yah. I know they didn't. It was because when we were with them, on their land or their lakes, we went by their laws. We respected them. For instance, it was forbidden to put fish cleanings in a lake. They allowed no smoking in the timber and asked a stranger to put his smoke out. When they picked blueberries you never found a crushed one. They never stepped on any. They called white pickers cattle, they were so clumsy.

"And, say! You never tasted fish like those Indian women fried it. They used a deep cast iron skillet filled over halfway with hot grease. The fish were put in and turned over and over. I dream about that fish yet. They often heaped onions on top of the venison. I never knew an Indian with stomach trouble. They didn't think pork was fit to eat. One time my brother Richard and I decided to stop by an Indian friend's house at breakfast time. We were invited to eat.

"Man, did it smell good! My brother got the first stack of pancakes; there was meat on the plate, too, that I thought looked kinda funny. Next, it was my turn. The squaw mentioned skunk grease sure fried plenty-good pancakes. About that time, I missed the fat dog that always laid behind the stove, I went out and set in the car until Richard came out. Told 'em my belly hadn't felt good all night."

"Besides games and fishing, what did you do for fun?" was my next question.

"Now, now, you are the dumb one! With all those pretty Indian girls around? We went to their dances, of course. At Onigum, an Indian village near Walker that had a big dance hall. The music was like that played everywhere, and could those gals dance! All dressed up in bright silk or some stuff like that. On a ladies' choice we got mobbed!" Imagining Alex at twenty was easy. He was still handsome.

"Those Indians were real boatmen. We used to go out on big old Leech Lake and sometimes storms hit. Bad ones. The main thing is to have a good companion who knows what to do quick, a big boat, and to quarter the waves. I loved the timberland, too. Worked at Effie and Ely, to name a few places. I had to fell the trees and skid them. We got paid by the stick, which was eight feet long. Some trees were ten sticks high and twenty-three inches in diameter. I worked for the Tomahawk Lumber Company from Wisconsin. They paid eight dollars a cord. Two men could cut six cords a day. We were furnished a horse. They had eighty-five dandies. In '45 I went to Washington where the damp weather jimmied me up.

"Oh, by gee, I got to tell you about Ole Moilenan, then you got me about talked out, I guess.

"Moilenan really needed a grindstone. Now, remember, there still was no Menagha or Sebeka at that time, so he had to walk the deer trail thirty miles to New York Mills. He made the trip, bought his grindstone, had an axle put in it, added handles, and loaded it with a hundred pounds of flour and some other stuff. Then he headed back down the deer trail with his grindstone wheelbarrow. Not so dumb, huh? He was a strong man.

"Father died when he was seventy-four. Mother lived into her eighties. Nope, I never came near getting married. Thought I'd give the ladies a break. I'd liked to have farmed, but I got rheumatism young, and then asthma and hay fever come along. I didn't really need 'em, but here they are."

Alex licked one finger and held it up to the wind. "'Goin' to rain before mornin', I betcha. My bones told me that before the wind did."

I thanked him and he walked me to the car.

It rained that night.

His fondness for liquor held up the paper!

Shanghai Chandler, one of the most colorful editors ever known, published Stevens County's newspaper, called *Frontier Business*, in Morris, Minnesota, in 1876.

Not much is known about Shanghai before he appeared in Morris, except that he had served in the Civil War. And he affected the garb and mannerisms of Buffalo Bill.

As editor, he wrote with reckless abandon and complete disregard for circumstances that might ensue. His sense of humor often saved the day – and his hide!

Shanghai attracted attention the minute he set foot in Morris.

He was dead broke, and applied for work at the home of Mr. and Mrs. House. Luckily, Mrs. House was making soap and needed help. When finished with the soap, Shanghai handed Mrs. House an itemized bill:

Setting up of leach .... 10¢
Carrying ashes .... 25¢
Loss of dignity $2.35

After trying his hand at a number of other odd jobs, he leased the local paper, then called the *Stevens County Reporter*.

Outspoken from the start, Shanghai's first issue of the paper explained that he had leased the paper from a "semblance of a man, W.H. Graves, a biped who proved to be a walking enigma, the puzzle being whether he was greater fool or knave." Shanghai enlarged the description by calling Graves a "deadbeat" and a "liar, with no more sense about running a paper than a donkey could repair a watch."

To customers, Shanghai proclaimed the price of the paper to be "Two Almighty dollars per year," always in advance. Shanghai was monarch in his printing shop, being sole proprietor, printer, star reporter, cub reporter and janitor. He never bothered to write his stories ahead of time. He set them directly into type.

Shanghai Chandler, maverick editor of Stevens County's FRONTIER BUSINESS, published the paper in Morris, MN. Copies of the colorfully-edited paper were long kept on file in the Morris Armory. Unfortunately, the Armory burned in 1969.

Often Shanghai's fondness for liquor held up delivery of the paper. On these occasions, he explained that printing had been held up for important news that failed to come in.

Morris' citizens decided one Fourth of July that Shanghai would be a proper orator for the day. His speech was classic. He appeared before his audience dressed in a swallow-tailed coat and silk tophat, with his beard shaved off. Instead of belaboring Bunker Hill and Gettysburg, he verbally took the hide off his many enemies, from one end of

town to the other.

He was slow to pay his bills, and when the proprietor of the Perkins Hotel told Shanghai, "I have a good mind to throw you out," the editor replied, "John, reason well before you do it." Shanghai stayed.

Still, he was most loyal to Morris and Stevens County, publishing articles filled with praise.

"Ye who seek homes in a clime and region fraught with every blessing, where health, fruits, fine scenery and fertile lands of easy cultivation may be purchased at government price...where no pestilent vermin are and crops never fail; go ye forth through all the earth in quest of such an ideal Eden and you'll wake to the realizing sense that ev-

ery rod of God's footstool is to be found at Morris, with a fine average farm for $200.00."

When he was dying, several of his friends gathered around the bed to ease those last moments. One of them felt Shanghai's feet, then pronounced in a subdued voice: "His feet are cold. The end must be very near."

Shanghai, struggling to one elbow, inquired if they had never heard of anyone dying with farm feet? Their answer was a mumbled "nope."

With a final smirk, the doomed man asked, "Then how about the early Christians who were burned at the stake?"

That was Shanghai Chandler's last jest.

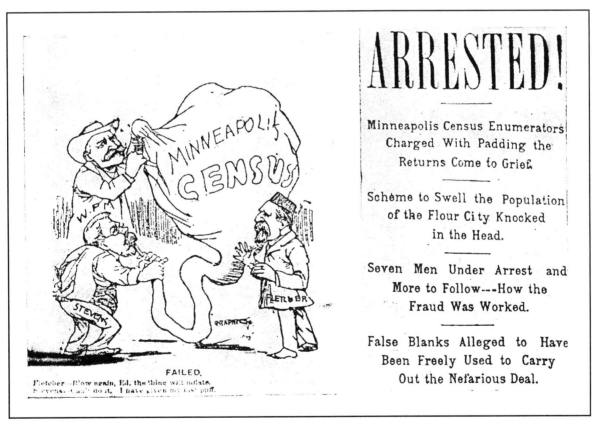

Cartoon and heading in Twin City Newspapers at the time of the St. Paul-Minneapolis Census Fight. From the "St. Paul Dispatch" of June 19, 1890 and the "St. Paul Daily News" of June 18, 1890.

When the University of North Dakota was nearly demolished!

On June 16, 1887, a severe wind storm entirely demolished the west wing of the main building of the University of North Dakota above the basement, blew down chimneys, and destroyed the cupola. Collections in the museum were almost a total loss. At a public meeting, held in Grand Forks the next day, resolutions were read voicing a very general sentiment in removing the institution to a site nearer the city rather than rebuilding.

This unexpected burden of expense placed upon them for repairs caused the board of trustees to send W.H. Roach to Bismarck to consult such a move with Governor Louis K. Church. With a communal sigh of relief, Roach was able to report at a meeting on June 28th, that the governor felt this might establish a dangerous precedent, and that the state would assist in every way possible. Upon hearing this report, the board decided to retain the site and repair the Main Building.

To meet these expenses a loan was authorized from local banks, not to exceed $10,000. The repair altered the original plan considerably: The cupola was omitted and the appearance of east and west gables much changed. A dormitory for young women was authorized, with an issue of territorial bonds not to exceed $20,000 in 1887. The name "Davis Hall" was selected in 1898 in memory of a much-loved preceptress.

The main building cost $30,000 in 1883, with $1,000 for incidentals and $400 for improvement of the grounds. An appropriation not to exceed

Group of Residence Halls
Views at the University of North Dakota

Science Hall and Woodworth Hall, University of North Dakota

$5,000 was made for salaries of the president and teachers.

The "new" building was opened on September 3rd, 1884. There was only one building on the campus, and that not fully completed. Living rooms for the faculty, dormitories for the students, a boarding department, class room, a library and museum, were all crammed into the same building. It was close quarters! During the first seven years, the student attendance grew from 79 to 151. The first graduating class in 1889 numbered a total of 20, receiving three degrees.

Ten years later the administration was put to a hard test when Governor Roger Allin vetoed the educational appropriations of the current legislative session. The university appropriation was reduced from $63,000 to only $15,000...hardly enough to complete the current college year.

Mass committees were formed that canvassed the area. Frantic appeals, asked "Shall the University of North Dakota close?" Closing the university would have been a calamity in many ways, among the worst of which would have been telling the world that North Dakota was either unwilling or unable to educate her sons and daughters! She has come through critical depression, crop failures, business disasters, as few other states have. She has been foremost in education. Will she now take her place farthest on the rear?

First, the faculty generously gave up 25 per cent of their salaries, a total of $8,250. Secondly, the citizens of Grand Forks subscribed $9,150, with the remainder coming from the counties of Walsh, Pembina, Burleigh, Nelson, Ramsey, Cavalier, Pierce, Ransom, Cass, and Steele.

This episode in the history of the University was not altogether unfortunate. It seemed to bind its constituency closer together, having sacrificed together for the general welfare of the whole.

By an act approved on April 28th, 1899, a fixed reserve for the State University was provided by a two-fifths mill tax. This fraction was changed by later enactments, but still serves its original purpose.

"Old Main", now Merrifield Hall, the first university building,
University of North Dakota.

"Lookout, Nancy!"

Mrs. Nancy Olson moved to Sauk Centre with her husband in 1859. In her words, she related, "I stepped to the door to throw out a washbasin of water and saw a large dog standing there. I put the dish down and was going out to call him. My husband yelled 'Lookout, Nancy! That's a big timber wolf, not a dog, and he is hungry. Close the door quick!' Well, I did. It was bright moonlight and I could see him just as plain. He was thin and half frozen, it looked to me. I never did that again!

"The upper part of the place where we lived that first winter was all in one room. I was the only woman among those who lived up there so we made a room with sheeting. Sometimes there was twenty people sleeping in that loft. We did not open windows because most windows in those days were not made to be opened anyway. The air poured in between the cracks and the snow blew in with gusto. It was not unusual to get up from under a snow blanket in the morning.

"I brought many pretty dresses and wore them, too. Those who came first, if they had money and were brides, were dressed as if they were in New York City. We had a dance one night in a little log "hotel". It was forty degrees below zero, and very cold only a few feet from the big stove. The women wanted to dance all the time and so set the table and put on the bread and cake before the company arrived. Five hours afterward when it was time to eat, they were frozen solid! The dish towels would freeze, too, as they hung on a line in the kitchen over this stove...while the stove was going!

"One morning, after we were keeping house, my husband said, 'I guess we have some spring company. You had better go and see them.' I did, and in our parlor was the biggest kind of an ox, standing there chewing his quid. He had just come on in through the open door to make an evening call. All kinds of animals ran at large then."

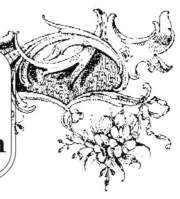

Pioneer doctors served homesteaders in wild, lonely region

Jenny Gossel

In all his life Pa never killed anything we didn't need for food. Yet he was a great believer in shooting arrows, and one of them saved my life.

I was fourteen the day Pa pulled his team to a stop at our back stoop and lifted from the wagon two blanket-clad figures. Ma opened the kitchen door, and a mighty gust of wind and snow swept them into the warmth of our kitchen. Spears of white frost clung to their blankets, and a trail of snow, already beginning to melt, followed them from the door to the stove. Ma opened the oven door with one hand and began to remove the blankets with the other.

"Here, Jen, lend a hand," she said to me, while motioning to the slightly shorter of the cocoons. A spindly little girl with scared, brown eyes emerged from one blanket, and a round-faced boy, badly in need of a haircut, almost fell out of the other. We had never seen the girl or boy before, and we knew everyone within a radius of many miles in those sparsely populated Minnesota backwoods.

Pa came in, stamping the snow from his four-buckled overshoes, and hung his sheepskin coat on a peg. Pa was six feet six in his sock feet.

"See," he said in a cheery voice, "I brought our children some playmates from town. I saw him look over my head at Ma and knew there was more to the explanation.

The boy's name was Ben; the girl's was Ruth. After downing a bowl of Ma's good beef stew, they fell asleep, still rosy from their long ride in the wagon. We helped Ruth into a nightgown that belonged to my younger sister Allie, while my nine-year-old brother Herb found pajamas for Ben. Ben shared Herb's big double bed with the cornshuck mattress. Ruth had to sleep in the bed with Allie and me. The addition made the bed full to capacity, it seemed to us, but after all Ben and Ruth were to be with us only a couple of nights.

The children's last name was Lothian. Their pa was the new doctor, just out of medical school. He had been sent to our little town to serve the homesteaders for many miles. Mrs. Lothian, Pa said, had caught a bad cold during the long trip from the city and had died yesterday of pneumonia. Dr. Lothian was beside himself with grief; he was in the new community, friendless and broke. Naturally Pa, being Pa, took most of our groceries to the doctor and offered to help in any way he could. That's when he bundled up the two youngsters and brought them home to us.

After six months had passed, I began to ask if Ben and Ruth didn't have relatives who could take them. Herb and Ben were quite comfortable, but three in our bed was exactly one too many. Besides, five of us had been splitting the money from the cream we sold – we had six cows – and now we had to divide it seven ways. Before, when Ma had time to sew, the things she made were for either Allie or me; now she had to make and patch clothes for Ruth and Ben too, so I had to do most of my own sewing.

Pa and Ma agreed that the kids were no trouble at all

Pa (Louie Gossell) at the age when this story took place.

and it would be better if they could stay with us rather than with relatives because their pa could come to see them sometimes. I didn't see how they could say that. Watching Pa try to stretch dollars that had already been strained to the breaking point turned me bitter, in spite of myself.

The doctor worked day and night. Ma filled him with some of her good cooking as often as she could. Once I saw Doc offer Pa a few dollars on the children's board. Pa refused, saying, "You get yourself a better horse, Son. If you could make your calls faster, maybe you'd get more rest." Often I'd heard Ma say, "In faith and hope the world will disagree; but all mankind's concern is charity." I wondered. When we had so little to spare, if anything, did Jesus still expect us to share?

Two more summers came and went. Ben was fair help by now around the farm, and Ruth had grown until Pa finally had to make her a cot of her own. Ben and Ruth were both healthy and happy. Then one day Doc drove in with an extra passenger in his buggy. He looked happier than I'd ever seen him. He helped a slender girl about his own age from surrey and introduced her to us as his wife. We were stunned speechless. Marrying was exactly what Pa had been wishing the young doctor would do all along.

Doc told us that another doctor was taking over in our town and that he had enrolled at the university for the coming quarter in order to get more schooling. The next morning we watched Doc and his new wife and Ruth and Ben depart. When the hind wheels of their new buggy were just visible through the cloud of fine dust that followed it, Pa pulled his straw hat low over his eyes and recited his favorite words of Longfellow:
" 'I shot an arrow into the air,
    It fell to earth, I knew not where ...' "
I tossed him an indulgent smile and went into the house.

Grandpa Gossell (a dear)

That year was a busy one. On a farm there is no end to the work. It seemed that I could never catch up and I was always tired. Allie and Herb could outwork, outrun, and even outwalk me. I also found excuses to evade the neighborhood parties I once had enjoyed. After a few months I became very weak and could no longer fool Ma that nothing was wrong. To please her I drank a succession of herb

teas and potions, the memories of which gag me to this day. Nothing helped and by fall I wheezed for every labored breath like a bellows; my heart felt as if it were trying to pound its way through my ribs.

One day Pa hitched up our horses, Dan and Nellie, and took me to Madison, a town twenty-five miles away, where there was a hospital. After a multitude of questions and much prodding, the Madison doctor referred us to a city specialist who made stops in Brandon, a town fifty miles farther away. "Your daughter has a large internal goiter. She has to have surgery at once," the specialist told Pa.

In those days surgery frequently meant death. I could think of at least a dozen persons who had been shipped home in pine boxes after undergoing nothing more serious than an appendectomy. Those who survived had faced long, slow periods of recuperation. The amount of money mentioned for the operation was more than Pa made in a whole year. I prayed to die.

"Who's the best doctor at taking out goiters?" Pa, not looking at me, asked in the tone he'd have used in inquiring about the future of seed corn.

"Dr. Arthur James in Minneapolis would be the best if he were available," the specialist said. "There's another fellow in a place called Milbank, South Dakota, who's getting himself quite a reputation for successful surgery."

"What's his name?" asked Pa, acting as if money was no object.

"Don't know that I've heard it," the specialist said. "But he's the only one there. I wouldn't wait to make an appointment, anyway." He looked at Pa in a funny way, and I knew he didn't think I'd last much longer without surgery. On the way home Pa asked the station master how much the fare for two to Milbank would be and came back to me to report. "The fare," he said, smiling the smile that could make the Statue of Liberty grin, "is within our means if I sell a few things when we get home."

The doctor's office in Milbank was plain, antiseptic, and empty. The doctor introduced himself as an assistant and took his time looking over the findings of the Bran-

don specialist. After a long, speculative look, he booked me for surgery the next morning. I hadn't heard Pa mention money at all. Dear old Pa. He supposed that everybody was as generous as himself. Even though I hadn't been around much, I knew it wasn't so. I tried desperately to think of something we had that wasn't already mortgaged; I failed.

The next morning after a worried, sleepless night, I was wheeled on a high cart into the operating room. My teeth chattered with terror, and my breath came in labored gasps from all the excitement. I couldn't help wondering what dying was like. Alien figures, swathed in white, slithered around the room. A sob escaped, in spite of myself. Then the head surgeon came in. He asked the nurse with the anesthetic to wait a minute, and he bent over until his eyes were only inches from mine. "Hello, Jen," he whispered.

**Dr. Lothian, well-known Milbank, SD
surgeon during the 1920's**

I recognized the top half of his face that the surgical mask hadn't covered and wheezed joyfully, "Doc Lothian! Oh, Doc Lothian, I'm dreaming."

"Not dreaming, Jen, and you're soon going to be good as new. I'll see to it myself." He exuded confidence and hope.

A month later I sat in Doc Lothian's office for the second time. I was still pale, but my breath came easily now, and my heart had quit pounding. I had spent three weeks in the hospital and the last week at Doc Lothian's home. Now Pa had come for me and this was good-bye. I held my breath while Pa asked for the bill.

"Bill? What bill?" Doc Lothian teased. "If anyone owes money it's me!" Then he said softly, "You helped me through the darkest days of my life. Remember?"

"I'm much obliged to you," Pa said gently. "Now I'd like to know how much the hospital charged, and then we'll have to catch our train."

"No hospital bill, either. I'm glad there was something I could do." Doc Lothian grinned at me. "Giving your Pa money is like trying to catch Niagara Falls in a dipper."

Going back home alive after a major operation was almost unheard of in our neck of the woods, so a sizable crowd was at the station to look me over. It was so good to be home.

That day was many years ago. Doc Lothian made an impressive name for himself in the early days of pioneering surgery, before going to join Pa and Ma in their celestial home across the Great Divide. There may be some who think it sheer luck that we found Doc Lothian just when we needed him most. I can't believe that. Doc Lothian was one of Pa's arrows that boomeranged. But like Pa used to say, before an arrow can come home, it has to be strung and shot. Pa shot that arrow into the air, like so many others, but with no thought of recompense years before it boomeranged to save my life. Ma was right: *All mankind's concern is charity.*

illustrated by jim padgett

Was there a Nininger?

It's December 1, 1856. Visualize a city, four miles north of Hastings, Minnesota, with a population bigger than that of New York City.

The city is Nininger, named after the man who owned the land, and it claims a population of 4,981,947 – 89,379 more people than live in New York City!

Credit, if there be any, for such a gigantic city goes to Ignatius Donnelly, Minnesota orator, public servant, businessman and author of *"The Immegrant Aid Journal,"* official publication of Nininger.

Donnelly's inspiration for "building" a city that would rival the great cities of the world came from a long-ago conversation between the Greek statesman Themistocles and a soldier:

"Dost thou know how to play the fiddle?" asked the soldier.

"No," answered Themistocles, "but I understand the art of raising a little village into a great city."

Confident he could do as much, he authored *"The Great Cryptogram,"* an epistle describing Minnesota in glowing terms. (Despite the enthusiastic description, Donnelly never saw Minnesota until after the book was off the press.)

Every page of *"The Great Cryptogram"* was an idealistic description of what was to be expected of the Territory of Minnesota. "Do not stop in Illinois," he warned, "lest you will be met not only by the Illinois Central Railroad but a severe fever and ague as well!" Iowa, he claimed, was crawling with pesky land speculators who "infest the state like famine."

The first issue of his publication was printed in both English and German. It also recorded that the Atlantic had been crossed in 36 hours in a new invention – very close to Charles Lindbergh's flight time (33-1/2 hours) to Paris 71 years later. Donnelly noted, too, that the last trip to the moon had taken seven months, and the next trip was expected to take less time.

Undoubtedly Minnesota's most proficient salesman,

**Ignatius Donnelly
The Sage of Nininger**

Donnelly also wrote, "Behold, then, the Promised Land before you; a climate of which poets have long sung...lovely in summer; more luxurious and infatuating in winter...a clear, still and invigorating cold...the air sparking with diamonds, the sun shining like a July day in a cloudless sky...stars sparkling as stars never sparkled before."

It worked. People flocked into Nininger.

Residences, mills, stores, saloons, blacksmith shops and factories were built. Lawyers', doctors' and dentists' prac-

tices thrived. Donnelly himself built a $10,000 home there, modeled after George Washington's Mount Vernon and Thomas Jefferson's Monticello.

Lots went from $5 to $20 each, and the city became associated with St. Paul, known as the "Nininger and Donnelly Addition".

Then, something happened. Few, if any, know just what caused Donnelly's dream city to dwindle. When the town folded, Donnelly closeted himself almost exclusively in his mansion for the rest of his life. There he turned out reams of manuscripts that, for the most part, remain unread.

Editor's note: Were there really 4,981,947 residents in Nininger in 1856? That figure is as difficult to authenticate as it is to refute. Official Census figures indicate phenomenal growth throughout the territory, then state, of Minnesota between 1850 and 1860. Yet, statistics for the intervening years are sketchy. It's possible the size of Nininger was a product of Donnelly's well developed imagination. But that's just as difficult to document. You decide.

The Kensington Rune Stone

Amos Brown:
Farmer/artist

One day after Amos Brown finished the light chores he was doing around the farm, he came in, ripped a page off the calendar and started to draw. Everyone was surprised but Amos. Why should he think that he could not draw when he had never tried?

Amos was born in Iowa in 1897. He moved to Verndale from Iowa in 1921. He and his wife, Phoebe, raised Helen, who now lives in Park Rapids, and Margurite, who lives in California, and Milton, who still lives on the home farm.

The growing crops, his cattle and nature, along with things pertaining to them, claimed Amos's interest and time. He just simply was satisfied and liked what he was doing.

Amos served in World War I and held jobs in Iowa and South Dakota. He belonged to the Verndale Methodist Church and was assessor for Aldrich Township for many years.

During all of these years, Amos never exhibited an interest in pictures or people who painted them. Reading, when he had time for it, some hunting, his family, farming, and a card party now and then filled his days. While

Amos was never the life of the party, he had a sense of humor that stayed alive until his death at almost 94.

Amos was an average-sized man, neither too fat or too thin. His was an even temperament with few mood swings to make his life either a heaven or hell. Stress? It has always been a part of life and always will be. Maybe knowing how to cope played a part in Amos's longevity.

One picture drawn on the back of a calendar with a stub pencil produced more sophisticated equipment once the family knew about it. He was set up with acrylic paints and a sort of easel as time went on. Amos was a natural, primitive artist that painted what he saw from wherever he was. When his wife had surgery for cataracts in Fargo, the tone of his paintings changed along with the view outside their motel room window.

A bout with that miserable disease called shingles slowed him down when it claimed the sight in one eye. Even so, he still painted anything he wanted to keep by putting it down on paper. Unlike Grandma Moses, Amos's pictures have depth, with straight roofs and chimneys. Some artists paint best at a particular time of day in certain light. Amos painted whenever, wherever he saw something he wanted to record or remember.

Paintings by Amos Brown were never so much as offered for sale or in a contest. He painted because he loved to do it. His pictures ended up in the hands (and on the walls) of family and friends. Amos enjoyed painting until he was 90, when he had to have a leg amputated.

Amos did not only preach the Christmas message of "Goodwill to Men" – he lived it. A picture painted in 1984 when he was 87 was turned into prints by his family and given to Shady Lane Nursing Home staff as a Christmas gift. Christmas was a season he especially enjoyed.

I'm betting most of us who worked at the nursing home still have ours.

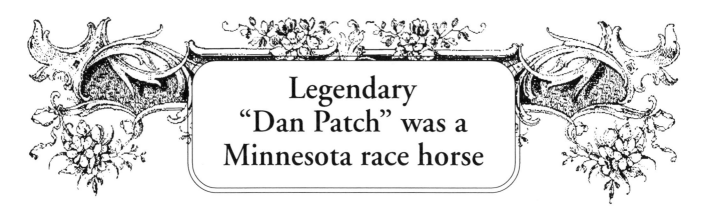

Legendary "Dan Patch" was a Minnesota race horse

Pacers are headed for Canterbury Downs, an event that brings to mind the most beloved pacer of all time – Dan Patch.

It was on September 6, 1906, that Dan Patch raced to establish the record mile – 45.91 feet per second – in 1:55 minutes at the Minnesota State Fair. A record that was to stand until 1945, then broken again. The current pace in a 1:49 mile.

The day Dan Patch broke the record a capacity crowd of 90,000 arose as one with a roar that rocked the stands to help cheer him on to victory.

Dan Patch was a deep-chested, clean-limbed mahogany bay stallion. A shapely head, held high with ears pointed forward, sported a white star in the middle of his forehead. He stood sixteen hands high, with the sweetest of dispositions. And how he loved to race!

Will Savage, owner of Savage Stock Farms near Minneapolis, was the owner of Dan Patch. The town of Hamilton was renamed "Savage" in honor of this operation with a horse of world renown in its stable. Dan Patch's popularity and recognition everywhere was augmented by the 8,000 miles, many by air, that he traveled each year during his racing career. This included several foreign countries and most states at one time or another.

Mr. Savage tried to have Dan Patch's races over by Christmas, at which time he was returned to the elaborate stable with its 160-foot wings, 40-foot alleys, lighted by 8,400 windows. There was also a half-mile covered track, the only one anywhere of its kind, with a tree bark surface that did not freeze during a Minnesota winter. In this way he was kept in racing trim. Dan Patch obviously lolled in his 26-foot square stall, waist deep in straw.

Murray Anderson was one of those responsible for Dan Patch's safety and care during many of his trips. "He didn't care how he traveled as long as he knew there would be a race at the end of the line. However, he refused to go anywhere without stablemates; his pals, or several mascot dogs he allowed to ride on his back, also along," Murray recalled.

During the years Murray lived at Shady Lane Nursing Home in Wadena, his eyes never failed to glisten with tears whenever he recounted the demise of the horse he loved.

Dan Patch was an incurable ham. At first glimpse of a camera in a crowd he instantly went into a pose: head up, ears pricked high, with one foot in the air, his white star pointed directly at the lens, seemingly saying "Go, ahead, folks, adore me!" He reveled in the triumphant strains of a brass band flanked by cheering crowds and pranced for their benefit.

At the age of twenty, Dan Patch joined the elite horseflesh that had already become history.

"I held that magnificent head to the last, thinking it might comfort him," Murray would say, reaching for his handkerchief.

Several days before Dan Patch's unexpected death on July 11, 1916, Will Savage entered Hillcrest Hospital with an illness from which he was expected to recover. Upon learning of the death of the pride of his life, the apple of his eye, he had a massive heart attack that took his life 32 hours later at the age of 57.

It is said that Will and Dan Patch were buried the same afternoon – Savage in Lakewood Cemetery; Dan Patch laid to rest beneath the branches of a tree that had long provided shade on a knoll that caught every breeze in the corner of the pasture from where Dan Patch had watched

the Minnesota River flow by many pleasant hours.

Dan Patch had been put to stud years before and while he produced many promising offspring, none attained the accomplishments of their sire, who still lives in the hearts of horsemen the world over.

The Dan Patch Story can be read in a book written by Fred Sasse.

Anderson, affectionately called "The Dan Patch Man" at Shady Lane, died several years ago. His only daughter, Annebelle, and her husband Merle Rickers reside in Wadena.

THE HORSE REVIEW SHOWS DAN'S WELCOME TO MINNEAPOLIS AT THE TIME HE WAS PURCHASED BY MR. SAVAGE.

Municipal Demonstration upon Dan Patch's Arrival in Minneapolis in December, 1903

Little Crow:
Fierce or friendly?

No one knew the two sides of Little Crow's personality better than Mrs. Gideon Pond. For her, either image – fierce warrior or enthusiastic student – was quite believable. The first time she met him, in 1851, was during her first marriage to Robert Hopkins.

It was a bright morning and Mrs. Hopkins had just finished tidying up the tiny, second-floor room of a log house owned by Dr. Williamson, Lac qui Parle County, Minnesota. She got out her writing materials, then sat down at the table to write to folks back East. How, she wondered, could she possibly describe the beauty of Lac qui Parle (Medeiadam), known by the Indians as "the lake that speaks in two tongues," because of a remarkable echo that haunted that particular lake.

Mrs. Hopkins had written no more than a few lines when something, a shadow or squeaky floorboard perhaps, made her drop her pen and whirl to face the door at her back.

There stood one of the most gruesome figures imaginable! Terrified, she forced herself to seem composed and unruffled.

The features were unmistakably Sioux. One half of the Indian's face was painted black the other half red, with white streaks running across both cheeks. A band around his head bristled with many large feathers, each signifying the death of an enemy. Mrs. Hopkins knew about the custom and shuddered.

Without coming closer or saying anything, the Indian left when he saw Mrs. Hopkins, determined to ignore him, shakily resume her writing.

That was Mrs. Hopkins' first encounter with the famous leader of the Sioux uprising in 1862.

Soon after this episode, Mr. Hopkins, a missionary, died while bathing in the river. Several years later, Mrs. Hopkins married Mr. Gideon Pond, an educator. Again, Mrs. Hopkins-Pond's path crossed that of Little Crow.

Mr. Pond became interested in trying to civilize Little Crow, a fine, tall, slender and handsome fellow. He had a pleasing singing voice and learned to read and write. Hard as he tried, however, Mr. Pond was never able to teach him to read music.

Not long after the lessons had been concluded, the Ponds moved to Traverse de Sioux (Minnesota). Years later, stories of the fearsome Little Crow reached their encampment. He was the leader of the Sioux uprising, the massacre that took the lives of several hundred white men, women and children on the Minnesota frontier in 1862.

As stories of Little Crow's latest atrocities reached Mrs. Pond, she had only to remember her first encounter with him to find them very believable. Why he took to Mr. Pond to the degree he did remained a puzzle.

Little Crow
The sketch was made by Mayer in 1851 at the Treaty of the
Traverse Des Sioux. Notice the calumet in his hand.

First bloodshed in the Sioux Uprising.

SURVIVORS WHO WERE AT THE TRAVERSE DE SIOUX AT THE TIME OF THE TREATY IN 1851. Mrs. Richard Chute, General William D. Le Due and Mrs. Gideon Pond, Mrs. Morris is standing by General Le Due. Taken at a celebration given in their honor July 17, 1914, by the Old Trails Chapter, at the home of Mrs. W.M. Savage.

When *"a thrill of horror convulsed the city"* of Moorhead;

The ghastly murder of a mild mannered doctor!

Special Story by Steve Tweed

The nights had become suddenly cooler, as they always did in western Minnesota during early September. The town was Moorhead, a burg of no more than 3,500, which boasted 45 full throttle, strong whiskey saloons – some with "soiled doves" for sale in adjacent bordellos. Stragglers from card games and glassy-eyed stare downs, from solitary drinking bouts and roistering gangs could be heard whooping and yelling oaths in the crisp autumn air.

Near the old Main Avenue bridge, on the Fargo side of the Red River, muggers waited in the darkness to knock off the shambling, staggering drunkards who sneaked back nightly to their dry Dakota town. Police reports suggested an average of one assault per night, sometimes more, when the drunks were thick as mosquitoes and the pickings good after pay day.

A couple blocks south of Main Avenue, near the present sight of the Moorhead Library, the now customary shouts and moans of more distant revelers were drowned out by a loud bashing sound, a series of thick, dull thuds and an ugly cracking noise which sounded like the snapping of wood… or bone. A young woman, returning to her home and unable to immediately get inside, heard the cruel, smacking noises from her screened porch, but refused to believe a murder was underway.

A moment later, when her father joined her on the porch, they listened as more commotion seemed to come from the darkness across the street. This time, as they later described it, they "heard some vicious striking of trees and buildings with a heavy club as a person (or thing) was passing along."

Moments later, Dr. Thrond S. Egge, aged 50, was discovered by a couple of brothers, Harry O. and Leroy Larson of Moorhead. Soon the gloomy corner was a scene of milling onlookers and police. The murderer was gone, leaving behind the victim of the community's most grizzly and horrific crime to date. The Moorhead Independent would recount:

When attacked, Dr. Egge was evidently on his way home, and was riding his bicycle. The doctor was carrying his medical case, wore his glasses, and his gloves were on his hands. The attack and murder occurred within 50 feet of the corner of Sixth Street and Second Avenue, almost directly opposite a new house in the course of erection for O.C. Beck. Dr. Egge's face was beaten in a horrible manner, and there is every indication that the first blow, which was across the top of the bridge of the nose, killed the victim. The latter's nose was beaten flat and the face was covered with ugly cuts and there were deep lacerations under the chin. The condition of the face and body of the doctor is said to have pointed plainly to the fact that the victim's head was beaten up after the fatal blow was struck.

The following day the Moorhead Weekly News would run a sub headline screaming that "The Whole City is Dazed With the Horror and Atrocity of the Crime," followed by this lead-in: "A thrill of horror convulsed the

city at close to midnight Monday night…"

And so the whispers began, as lights went on from one end of town to the other, and neighbors awoke to the news of a ferocious attack and killing near the rim of their little downtown Gomorrah. Police wagons slowly rolled by hapless pick pockets and Murphy men who clustered around the bridges under gaslights. Jaded from bar brawls and mean human vice, the Moorhead cops coldly scanned the faces of the shuffling rabble they knew so well, looking for the furtive, desperate face of a killer – but to no avail.

But an officer Erickson, enraged by the crime and fueled with adrenaline, found a blood-stained wagon wrench on a coal wagon which stood at the Fifth Street crossing of the Northern Pacific Railroad tracks. The murderer had taken the tool, which held a "doubletree" to the tongue of the wagon, had used it on his victim, then returned it, leaving a bloody handprint plastered on the wagon's side as he steadied himself.. In the moments to come, excited, breathless accounts of a barroom feud gone out of control were spilled to the senior police officers by the barflies who were willing to talk.

It seemed that Dr. Egge, described by the papers as "esteemed among all classes and industrious in his profession", had been tippling in one of the downtown gin mills. After being challenged one too many times by a man he considered a nuisance and common ruffian, he finally turned and grabbed the man, shoved him roughly and ended up hurling him into a corner. The man who crashed to the floor, skulking in shame at his humiliating defeat, was Frank Kethman. Later that night he would be roused from his bed by police and charged with the crime of murder.

And so it was in the little town of Moorhead.

Nightfall brought on carousing and mischief; the morning sun revealed barkeeps rolling out their awnings and setting up straight shots for the painfully hung over regulars. Some would claim that bodies regularly washed up on the banks of the Red. Stories persisted about sots who had been flung into the river by bouncers, or dropped

Newspapers offered florid prose covering the vice beat

American newspapers at the turn of the century were rife with colorful, often poetic sounding prose, and the tabloids of Fargo and Moorhead were no exceptions. Imagine a paper in our era of tone-deaf, factual news writing coming up with a paragraph like this one from the long defunct Moorhead Weekly News:

The News is informed by men who seem to know, that gambling is now prevalent in this city in a half dozen or more places, and that a gang of not less than fifty of what are termed "tin horn gamblers" infest the city. It can be said to the credit of some of the proprietors of saloons that the News has talked with, that they are earnestly in favor of breaking up this unlawful and demoralizing business. They well say that it attracts to our midst the worst elements of society – men who would not hesitate to rob, outrage or murder, if the inclination should seize them or it should fit their purposes. There can be no more demoralizing or degrading business or practice than gambling, and the permanent residents of Moorhead owe it to themselves and their families to see that the law is invoked to rid the town of this vice. The saloons are sufficiently evil, corrupting and debauching, without these adjuncts of Satan.

Though the papers were critical of saloon keepers when it suited them, they could also ladle out syrupy words for favored barmen (who probably advertised or even bought a free shot glass or two). The following comes from the Moorhead Citizen in 1911:

Higgins-Aske Co., have had a tile floor laid in their place of business at the north bridge and have also made many other improvements. They now have the longest straight bar in the state and the only bar in the United States that has three eight drawer cash registers. On account of their increase in business they were compelled to make these improvements. They now have the neatest and most up-to-date bar room in the country. There is nothing too good for Messrs. Higgins and Aske and they are doing their best to cater to the public in the best possible manner.

The Fred Ambs Saloon on what is now Center Avenue between 4th and 5th streets about 1898. This was one of the fancier bars in town, catering to well to do patrons, not the flotsam of petty thieves and drifters.
Flaten/Wange collection, Clay County Historical Society

August J. Rustad's saloon on the north side of Main Avenue, right on the bridge. This particular joint was built as close to the river as possible to lure Fargo clientele in before they even set foot on Minnesota soil! It was constructed to replace another bar that had burned down in 1904.

Flaten/Wange collection, Clay County Historical Society

Finally, there was the matter of the whisky rafts which wrought havoc on workers and their families up and down the Red River Valley. Getting high on the job a hundred years ago rivaled anything Timothy Leary would later hatch with his "tune in, turn on, drop-out" philosophy for the Sixties psychedelic generation. Look at this horrified response to a "miserably wicked" practice as found in the Moorhead Weekly News in 1892:

It is stated by farmers living along the Red River north of Moorhead that the whisky rafts have played havoc with their harvest and threshing hands. It has been an intolerable nuisance and of pecuniary damage to the farmers, as the men have become intoxicated at times when most needed, and have gone off or been unfit for work. There is also another way of reaching the farm laborers during the threshing season out on the farms at long distances from the towns. Men driving buggies distribute liquor to the farm hands. They do it stealthily and go from farm to farm so speedily that is impossible to intercept them, as the mischief they do does not show itself until some time after their visit, when they are beyond reach. What a miserably wicked and unholy an employment this is for a being to be engaged in.

In 1915, by vote of a majority of the voters in a county election, Clay County declared itself against the sale of liquor within its borders. Moorhead's riotous days were over, for the moment, until bootlegging set in. The Moorhead Weekly News ran a headline which read: Out in a Blaze of Glory: Biggest Crowd in History of City Thronged Front Street… Shooting of Firecrackers, Roman Candles, Rockets, Ringing of Bells, Singing and Shouting Marked the Closing Last Night.

One of the biggest crowds that ever thronged the streets of Moorhead, both in autos and on foot, witnessed the closing of the saloons of Moorhead shortly after 11 O'Clock last night.

For the past two or three weeks the dealers have been busy disposing of their stocks, and with one or two exceptions, were out of wet goods. When the places started to close up, and those inside were compelled to go out, singing and shouts rent the air… at both bridges the crowds seemed loath to leave for home, and the refrain "How Dry I Am" was taken up and shouted and sung to the echo.

through trapdoors into the muddy, swirling eddies. Throughout the day, tipplers rolled in and out of the 45 taverns, some pounding back three fingers of dark amber fire water every hour… hour after hour. Frank Kethman, the dark and brooding carpenter, seems to have committed his crime at the tail end of a daylong binge. At the scene of the crime, he left behind a Labor Day parade badge worn by carpenters who had marched twelve hours before the attack on Dr. Egge. Woozy and disoriented, Kethman had sat on a curb just blocks from the assault, head buried in his hands, telling a cop he didn't know how he would make it home.

Perhaps the murder of Dr. Egge was committed in a state of blackout. We will never know. Muggings, brawls and physical attacks were pretty common in turn of the century Moorhead, and the murder of the gentle doctor was probably an inevitable statistic. How many beatings or robberies could emanate from little Gomorrah before someone died? In any event, the Egge murder and other perceived outrages later led to the downfall of "rule by rum" in Moorhead.

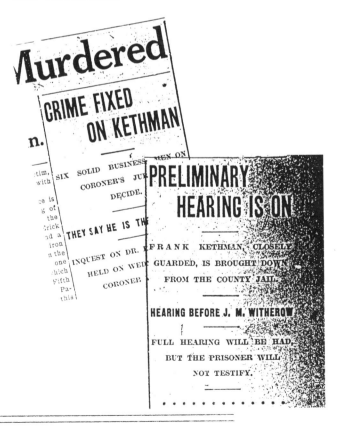

The view is to the north on 4th street from Main Avenue. Ralph's Corner is visible at the extreme left... in fact, all the businesses on the left side of the street were saloons.

Flaten/Wange collection, Clay County Historical Society

Another view to the north, from the present Sportland location. Main Avenue is in the foreground – all buildings on the north side of Main were saloons.

Flaten/Wange collection, Clay County Historical Society

When Will Rogers said

Moorhead was
"the wickedest city in the world"

Special story by Gertrude Knutson

It may seem strange to a citizen of Moorhead today that originally the founding fathers deliberately promoted saloons—as a major industry! That's because saloons would be a lucrative foundation for the economy. But that's exactly what happened with the new town of Moorhead, which had an excessive number of saloons for its small size. The industry boom lasted from approximately 1878 to 1915.

Not all saloons were equal. Some were fancier and sturdier than others. The more serious owners made their saloons enticing to prospective customers. For instance, the White House had a summer garden outside, and on the inside sported electric fountains, solid oak features and pink frame windows. The Higgins-Aske Co. had a tile floor, "the longest straight bar in the state" and the "only bar in the country that had three 'eight drawer' cash registers. Hass' place had four hundred electric lights; Rustad's saloon featured brass footprints leading to the door…and Ed Wilson's proudly claimed a $200 mirror!

The saloon owners were not content for their customers to come to them, but would dispatch rafts on the rivers or buggies on the roads to sell whisky to farm hands (who then became too drunk to work the rest of the day – much to the chagrin of their bosses).

The city's special accommodation in making life easier for the saloon owners led to corruption of some of the city officials. Early on, a police chief and city treasurer were fired for embezzlement. There is also the suspicion that some of the saloon owners bribed officials so as to stay open after hours and on Sundays, though there was legally no proof. The mere fact that many did stay open after midnight and on Sundays leant support to that suspicion.

The most noticeable corrupting phenomenon was the establishment of houses of "ill repute" and the presence of streetwalkers. Sometimes the city would have houses torn down, only for the prostitutes to find other houses. Other times, the court would fine the prostitutes and tell them to leave town (which they sometimes did) but on the whole it was a difficult trade to abolish.

In saloons, the ladies of the night often served as decoys, to lure the suckers into situations where they would easily be robbed.

The Moorhead News reported that a brutal assault took place in the Tivoli Theater involving a Frenchman by the name of Timolien Despond, who was an industrious carpenter from Wild Rice, North Dakota. Unfortunately, he had (on occasion) a weakness for drinking too much liquor.

On the evening in question, he strolled into the theater, having on his person $156. Being half intoxicated, he was beguiled into a private box, where he met a woman, presumably an "actress". He then purchased a dollar bottle of beer for each of them.

After being in the box for some time, he became insensible, and remembered nothing until he came back to his senses and found he was the only occupant of the box. His money was gone, with the exception of a few small silver pieces in one of his pockets. His watch and chain were also missing. Despond's head and face were covered with blood. Two of his front teeth were knocked out, his lips were split open, and he had suffered a deep wound

on his head which a physician (Dr. Awty) claimed was inflicted with a bottle.

Despond said he was drugged and assaulted. He was taken to the Moorhead station house for the night, and in the morning was liberated and went to Dr. Awty's office for his wounds to be dressed. He then swore out a complaint against a John Mannis, whom he claimed had assaulted him. Mannis was arrested and pleaded guilty before Justice Syron and was fined $25, with an additional $5 tacked on for the doctor's fee. Mannis was not sure he could even pay the fine, but the news writer figured that would be solved: he wryly suggested that Mannis would go back to the dive to wait for his next victim.

The News complained that Mannis was merely charged with simple assault, when he should have been charged with murderous assault —having used a bottle, (a lethal weapon).

The News further believed the affair was "smoothed over." Although the city attorney was called upon to draw up a complaint, he was never called upon in court, since the Justice said the prisoner had pleaded guilty, and thus a hearing was not necessary. The News maintained that the house – the Tivoli Theater- ought to be responsible for the loss of Despond's money and watch, and also added that there was a loud demand that the Tivoli should be closed entirely.

Ordinary women were not supposed to enter saloons, but there were exceptions, possibly because some watering holes were dining places such as the House of Lords and the Midway Buffet. There was an unusual exception when a bar owner had his wife fill in as a bartender: it was said he could get by with it because of being German, and not Scandinavian.

So – if a saloon customer met a female on the premises, it would be naïve not to know she was a prostitute and that she was there to steal in more ways than one. Police Chief Malvey raided the streetwalkers and they were told that their solicitations would not be tolerated. Occasionally the madams were brought to court and fined (and sometimes jailed) but often the judges would suspend the

sentences if the prostitutes left town – which they usually did.

According to the papers, comparatively rare "colored" people were once also involved in prostitution in Moorhead. Police Chief O. Laughlin and city attorney Rustad raided a house where "a hilarious beer party was in progress. The officers arrested a colored couple and another colored woman, and a white man who was pulled from under the bed." (Moorhead Weekly, Aug 17, 1911). The paper went on to say: "It seems that a regular service by row boat was furnished across the river from the Fargo side to the joint… The entire outfit was bundled out of town, with a long term sentence hanging over them should they ever be picked up again in Moorhead."

A woman by the name of Scotch Nell was arrested for being drunk and disorderly on the streets January 21, 1901. But after "making life interesting for the police of Fargo and Moorhead" she decided to reform and left for St. Paul to enter the House of the Good Shepherd, "under the care of Mrs. Kelly of the Salvation Army." It has been said that contrary to popular fiction stories of prostitutes turning over a new leaf, such events were not very common, so the story of Scotch Nell stands out as an exception to the rule.

Perhaps the only madam who publicly projected a warm heart was Kittie Raymond, who ran a house of ill repute. It so happened that one of her girls – Kate Skinner a.k.a. Stella Moore – dropped dead on the sidewalk in front of the Grand Pacific Hotel. She was just 19 years old. Her body was taken back to the Beck and Wright Funeral Home where it would be embalmed until her mother could be found. Kittie wanted the "best" for her girls. The fact that the mother's whereabouts was not known shows the classic family estrangement, often the cause of young women going astray.

There was another corrupting element which, while not encouraged by the saloons, never the less existed in them. The Moorhead Weekly relates the following classic gambling tale:

"A harvest hand had been enveighed into playing with

a gambler. The gambler bet $10 without even looking at his cards. The thresher had four "fours" and raised the bet another $5. The gambler called him and on a show of hands held four kings.

The thresher pulled a revolver, demanded his money, charged it was a put up game… and fired.

No one was hurt.

Chief Sullivan says some arrests were made at the saloon (Hanson and Peterson's) for disorderly conduct, but no complaint was made alleging shooting or swindling. The parties were all fined."

Apparently gambling was fairly prevalent in Moorhead in half a dozen places and a gang known as the tin horn gamblers were not popular with the local saloon owners (probably because of violence involved and also because the gamblers took money away from saloons).

Diemert/Murphy's "family liquor store" about 1905. The Old North Bridge is visible to the extreme right. Flaten/Wange collection, Clay County Historical Society

Never the less, stealing of various types seems to have been encouraged, or at least not policed as much as it should have been.

One reader of the news suggested that a drunken customer could hand a cashier a ten or twenty dollar bill and be cheated when given his change, since he would be too drunk to notice. It seems likely that this type of stealing went on frequently.

In fact, stealing was so common that citizens expected to be stolen from. According to the Midweek News, when a visitor to the FM cities had gone too often to the bars and ended up under arrest in Moorhead after he sobered up, he was immensely happy to be jailed, for he still had $1,357.20 in cash, a gold watch and chain and some German paper money on his person. He could have easily lost them to a thief in his drunken condition.

Danger was everywhere. A prominent physician, Dr. Thrond Egge, who had a drinking problem, had quarreled with a fellow customer in a saloon and was later killed by that same companion.

Sometimes the saloons themselves were the object of violence. Two brothers – Gust and Ed Johnson – had been arrested for stealing clothing from Wilson's saloon. When they were released from jail, they went back to the saloon and smashed a $200 mirror. Another thief hid in an empty whiskey barrel until the joint (Waldron and Rief's) was empty – and then proceeded to rob it!

Occasionally the police actually raided a saloon such as the New Central House, where they knocked down the doors to locate contraband goods (hidden in the closet of the parlor-bedroom in the back). The Schneiders, who owned the saloon, were fined $25 or 30 days in jail, which would be suspended if they left town (which they did). Violence even affected public transportation, in that if a would-be customer refused to take a hack (cab) home he would risk being assaulted.

The police once dealt with a man who claimed to have been robbed of $25 in a saloon, but the police were dubious since the saloon was known to be orderly. The real story was that the man had spent 15 cents and had de-

sired to blackmail the saloon.

In nearby Sabin, a group of women (no doubt inspired by Carrie Nation) took hatchets to a local store that sold the "red liquid" and smashed every bottle in front of the unhappy owner.

And while selling the whisky was generally confined to within the saloons, the effect of that liquor consumption spilled outside, where drunken men using fowl language accosted pedestrians and sometimes used firearms (which naturally frightened the public!) Intermingling with these drunks were the streetwalkers. It is no wonder that old women remembered that when they were young girls they were afraid to go to down town Moorhead in the day light. But my mother, as a schoolgirl, walked by these same saloons and later commented that the lumberjacks sang beautifully. (Some of the saloons were open 24 hours, although that was frowned upon).

Beyond the confines of the saloon buildings, the saloon owners influenced society in that their daughters came to school dressed in silks and satins – in contrast to the homespun material worn by the other girls. Their sons would have new cars sooner than the other boys. Their houses were often bigger and more lavish than was ordinary.

One gets the impression that their money came easily and went easily, spent frivolously (like giving spools of silk thread for their cats to play with).

Nor did education seem as important to saloon owners as it did to the stolid Scandinavians, who built many churches and schools. However, the community noted that saloon owner Rustad sent his son to Harvard.

There must have been a certain lack of respect amongst the public for making money through liquor, for there was a tale about a prominent woman from saloon life. It was reputed that her long skirts and petticoats whispered "whiskey…whiskey… whiskey" when she walked down the church aisle. Her husband was said to have begun his upward climb cleaning spittoons, but he went on to wholesale booze, then finally big banking and real estate interests in Fargo.

The "Rathskeller on the Rhine" saloon about 1905, run by Thomas Erdell. The partially obscured house next door was connected to the Rathskeller by an infamous tunnel; talk of prostitution in these quarters persisted, and was perpetuated by the fact that this "house" never showed up on any city directories.
Flaten/Wange collection, Clay County Historical Society

Here is a view to the west on Main Avenue from 4th street. Ralph's Corner is on extreme right, the present Kirby's on the left. Saloons may be seen on the north side of the street, other businesses on the south side. Between 1910 and 1915.

Flaten/Wange collection, Clay County Historical Society

Probably the most hurtful aspect of the saloon industry was that husbands, fathers and sons stopped at the bards for drinks before they went home, and in many cases, spent either all or most of their money on booze… leaving nothing for their families to eat or wear.

There was a wife whose husband came home after stopping at a saloon. He brought only 10 cents worth of liver to feed a roomful of boarders. The wife was so angry that she went to the saloon and got her husband's check back!

Beyond the doors of the saloons, the air was filled with foul and obscene language, dirty smells and the occasional volley of gunshots. Such a lurid atmosphere, open to the public and quite legal, was vulnerable to attack from critics. And so a war began.

(However, the indignant public displayed schizophrenic behavior, objecting to the noise of the Salvation Army drums to the point that even the leader, Mrs. Kelly, was jailed. But this brave woman knew how to turn a lemon into lemonade – she managed to collect $50 for her cause in jail!)

The anti-saloon warriors arose from the churches, colleges, Salvation Army and the Women's Christian Temperance Union, which concentrated on educating the public about the dangers of alcoholism. Several ordinary citizens spoke before the mayor and aldermen. One of the strongest leaders in the opposition to saloons was Pastor Martin Anderson, who swore to rid Moorhead of the problem. He suffered verbal abuse and threats, and had his yard strewn with bottles… to the point that the chief of police offered him protection during night hours. Yet he survived to view his "victory over the Devil."

In 1915 the saloon era ended in Moorhead (even though the town voted to stay wet) when an election made Clay County dry. Moorhead had to abide by the vote.

So, the long sojourn of the saloons ended for the next 15 years, after which they returned, less in number and subdued.

For many years, one man, Joseph Kiefer, stood for the sale of liquor. He served as alderman for several terms and was elected mayor for one term. It was his philosophy that saloons were a legitimate way to earn a living, provided that the bars were run in an orderly and regulated way. He had owned a saloon as well as a wholesale liquor business, which he held until prohibition. He then purchased a livery stable, which eventually became a car dealership that his family ran for 50 years.

But other mayors and aldermen were often suspected of taking a cut from the saloon trade, although such claims were seldom proved legally. Part of the suspicion arose from police failure to get the saloons to close according to their contracts with the city of Moorhead

Prohibition failed to remove the sale of liquor in Moorhead as bootleggers began to make and sell booze regardless of the law. Many of them were in and out of jail many times, but that is a story for another time.

Sometimes prostitutes were reputed to be generous and warm hearted, and bootleggers had their virtues too. The Magnuson family of bootleggers adopted an orphan boy, and Mrs. Magnuson did right by him, sending him to Sunday school and public school. When the boy grew up, he went to the state of Washington, where he made a name for himself as a powerful senator from that state. He also provided a home for Mrs. Magnuson on an island off the coast of Washington in her old age.

It should also be noted that drunkenness remains even more of a hazard now than in the old saloon days, because today drunks drive cars and often injure or kill people. In cars, the drunk is invisible.

(I wish to thank Mark Peihl of the Clay County Historical Society who has generously allowed me to read and use the material available on the saloons. I also used A Century Together, a history of Fargo and Moorhead, and Trinity Lutheran's Centennial History 1882-1982. There were also personal family recollections – G.A. Knutson)

Out in Blaze of Glory

Biggest Crowd in History of City Thronged Front Street, First Avenue North and First Avenue South---Shooting of Firecrackers, Roman Candles, Rockets, Ringing of Bells, Singing and Shouting Marked the Closing Last Night.

One of the biggest crowds that ever thronged the streets of Moorhead, both in autos and on foot, witnessed the closing of the saloons of Moorhead shortly after 11 o'clock last night.

The closing came as a result of the county option election May 17, when by a majority of 1059 the voters of Clay county declared themselves against the sale of liquor within the boundaries of the county. Owing to the fact that the licenses of the Moorhead liquor dealers ran out June 30 and that a provision of the county option law prohibits the issuance of new licenses after a county option election the saloons had to close last night.

For the past two or three weeks the dealers have been busy disposing of their stocks, and with one or two exceptions were entirely cleaned out of wet goods. The House of Lords at the north bridge closed up at 7 o'clock, but the rest of the places ran the full limit to 11 o'clock.

When the places started to close up and those inside were compelled to go out, singing and shouts rent the air, accompanied by the shooting of firecrackers, Roman candles and rockets. At both bridges the crowds seemed loath to leave for home, and the refrain, "How Dry I Am," was taken up and sung and shouted to the echo.

Finally, as the truth seemed to dawn on the gathering that the "stuff was off" the crowds commenced to dwindle, and by 3 o'clock this morning had dispersed.

Detroit Lakes ace did us proud in B-29 Bomber

Everett (Jack) Viken, son of Mrs. Ole E. Viken, West Lake Shore Drive in Detroit Lakes, was raised in the area, mostly in the vicinity of the airport. To get a ride, or (oh, joy!) a lesson, he happily washed planes for weeks. This is how Jack learned to fly. His was an intense interest. He had nerves that refused to become rattled, wrapped in layers of common sense; something seldom found in a kid of fourteen.

A few years down the line, Jack became owner of first a Piper Cub, then a bi-plane. He paid for them doing barrel-rolls before grandstand crowds, flying a few feet above the ground...upside down...picking handkerchiefs off the end of sticks with propeller blades. People loved him.

On the no-no side of the ledger, Jack landed between cars and took off again on Highway 10, flew UNDER bridges, buzzed the police station. If a fine was involved, as it usually was, he sat it out. Money was for keeping up planes. Besides, there was "No better way to get chummy with the local gendarmes than shoot the breeze with them for a day or two at a time now and then," Jack claimed.

"Funny," he mused, "when most guys come home they give 'em a big parade. They gave me one when I sold my planes and LEFT!"

However, there is no record of Jack ever doing anything to cause anybody harm; just too much soup and vinegar. He left to join the air force.

Flyboy – one of Jack's favorite planes. He was also a pool and billards whiz.

Years later, during my first week of work at Shady Lane Nursing Home, I met Jack. He stood out in a solarium filled with people in rockers and wheelchairs or clutching canes and walkers. He was sitting next to a window, arms folded before him across his walker, eyes filled with longing at a patch of sky above the tree tops. I pulled up a chair, making some inane remark like, "A nice day, huh?" He turned black eyes on me with so withering a look it made my skin curl. Did I think he couldn't see that for himself, it said. He hated being talked down to, though I didn't mean it that way.

It took months to get conversation with Jack past sarcastic observations and caustic, cutting remarks. Here was a bitter man.

Jack must have been a stunner when he was twenty-five. He was still always neat at sixty-five. A photo of him working as a life guard was proof...black eyes and black hair, 6'2" tall at 180 pounds. Still handsome and intelligent, he was completely out of his element. Not another person in the entire area came close to "talking his language."

After months I finally convinced Jack that I was sincerely interested in his past and planes. Hadn't my husband worked as final inspector at North American Aircraft in Inglewood, California, even before Pearl Harbor? And he inspected Mustangs, Jack's favorite plane. Though he, like Chuck Yaeger, liked them best, he could and did fly anything up to and including B29s. An old newspaper picture showed a B17 with a huge hole in the fuselage with Jack squatting in it, smiling. "She'd got him home," he said with reverence. He came in with two engines out more than once. A couple of times most of his squadron had been shot down above the Pacific and lost. Jack's experiences were awesome – and true. He never bragged. Many times both wingmen, planes designed to fly on each side to protect Jack's plane with the bomb load, were shot down leaving him unprotected from the Jap Zero's. "I prayed for those below every time I signaled to my bombardiers to open the hatch an' let them eggs fly," recalls Jack.

Girls? Oooooh, yeah! Jack liked girls, alrighty! All colors and any size, over the entire Pacific Theatre. Jack was a "legs" man. What idiot, he wondered, put nurses in long-legged white pants? Shoulda been shot! While he admitted to having had lottsa girls, he had loved only one. "My pretty little wife. She died giving me a baby girl. Lives in Texas. Got three fine grandsons, too." It was after his wife died that Jack joined the air force.

Jack declared, "Women are dumb! Plain stupid! You wouldn't believe how they hung around our camps. A push over for any uniform without botherin' to find out who was in it. But not my wife. Wasn't in uniform when she fell in love with me. She never got to see my wings; all that fruit salad. Wouldn't have made any difference to her anyhow."

"Aw, Jack! You think I'm like that?" I asked.

"Well, I guess not ALL of 'em," he concedes, giving my knee a pat. I slap his hand to prove it.

Helping him find a comb in his drawer one day, I noticed several objects, tarnished black. Inspection proved them to be medals. I found three Distinguished Service Flying Crosses with their tiny props and five Oak Leaf Clusters each, Asian Pacific Fleet Medal, Sub-machine Gun Expert Medal, Expert Radio Operator and one for Radio Mechanic Medals, Korean Service Medal, Presidential Medal, plus others. He'd never counted nor taken care of them. He shot down 43 Jap Zero's with witnesses, and others no one saw that didn't count. His was the 1928th AACE Squadron. By the way, I checked these out with a veterans office. Jack was an ace.

I was overwhelmed. "Jack, I'm so proud of you!" I enthused.

"Proud!" he blazed. "Why? I just did what I was supposed to. You think I enjoyed killin' all them poor devils down there? Little babies, old people, others who didn't even know why there was a war. Anyhow, the guys who shoulda got those medals are dead. THEY was the aces. Now, get them things outta here! Throw 'em in the junk. I never asked for one or went to pick it up!" They were shined up and sent to his daughter. "Bombs don't always

land where they're supposed to, you know," he called after me.

Following the service, Jack flew as a Special Government Agent on the Mexican border for a few years. After that he hired out to Vultee-Vengeance of California as a test pilot. He loved the job and stayed twelve years. His foot and Chuck Yaeger's found themselves on the same bar-room rail many a time.

Twice Jack cracked-up his plane in all that flying...walking away both times. The last time hospitalized him for a few days. The car taking him home from the hospital had an accident that injured his spine and put him in a nursing home for the rest of his life. He never walked alone again.

Is it any wonder those black eyes held so much resentment? Bitter to the core.

Taking Jack outside was an experience. He'd look long at the sky with such yearning I wanted to cry. Then he'd say, "That's where it all is...the only place to be...way up there! Quiet. Peaceful, with this rotten old earth far far below. Nothin' but trouble down here. Many a time I wisht I'd just pulled the nose of my old Mustang up an' kept goin'!" I never heard anyone more sincere.

Jack was on his way to lunch, edging along with his walker, when his heart stopped. His body was returned to Detroit Lakes.

I like to think of Jack high up in the sky he loved so much, free at last of the miserable cords that bound him to an earth he detested, never had time for. Back up in his element.

☆ **New in Roominess** ☆ **Richness** ☆ **Quietness**
With still easier handling ☆ **A soft, quiet ride**
THE CAR TO KEEP YOUR EYE ON
* * Nov. 1939, P.J. * *   is the 1940 Ford!

De Luxe
FORD V·8
for 1940

IN A 1940 FORD *you get more room, greater quiet, a finer ride, easier handling, and a much more luxurious car than ever before. There are no less than 22 important 1940 improvements, including the following:*

Greater legroom, elbowroom; new seating comfort

New finger-tip gearshift on steering column (All models, no extra cost)

Improved soundproofing; quieter operation

Stunning new interior richness throughout

Self-sealing hydraulic shock absorbers

New front window ventilation control

New instrument panels; new 2-spoke steering wheel

Improved springing and chassis stabilizing on all 85 h.p. models

New Sealed-Beam headlamps; beam indicator on dash

And the *only* V·8 engine in any low-priced car!

Robbery of the century!

The Mankato (Minnesota) Board of Trade called a large meeting of citizens. They were looking for a scheme that would shoo business towards Mankato's main street and away from that of its competitor, Northfield.

As the meeting was being called to order, two horsemen rode into town at an easy trot. Without stopping, they rode out again.

Once out of town, the horsemen headed their horses towards a thicket at a dead run. There, waiting for them, were six accomplices. Pulling up short, one cowboy said, "Won't work. They were waitin' for us. How'd they find out? We'd be crazy to go through with it here!" The others nodded.

After a short discussion, all eight decided instead to ride on to Northfield – and the First National Bank.

Local post offices had pictures of the eight horsemen – Robert, James and Cole Younger, Jesse and Frank James, Clel Miller, William Stiles and Charlie Pitts.

It was broad daylight, September 7, 1870, when the first two men left the wooded area, five miles west of Northfield. They rode into town, tense smiles on their faces.

They hitched their horses to a rail in front of a drygoods store and lounged on boxes on the front walk. As three of the other men, equally unhurried, approached town from the opposite direction, the first two ambled towards the bank. The remaining outlaws placed themselves at strategic points along Main Street.

Meantime, a merchant by the name of Allen, having business to transact, tried to walk into the bank but was prevented entry by force. This tipped the outlaws' hand.

Allen dashed around the corner to spread the alarm. He alerted Dr. H.M. Wheeler, who had been half asleep in one of the chairs in front of his father's drug store. Wheeler rushed for the Dampier Hotel, opposite the bank. Stationed there, in a second story window with a gun and plenty of ammunition, he peppered and wounded Bob Younger.

J.L. Haywood, acting as bank cashier for that day, was killed when he refused to open the safe. H.E. Bunker was wounded by Pitts, while outside the other brigands, brandishing rifles, patrolled the streets on horseback, shouting commands and threats.

Allen, the hardware dealer who had first spread the alarm, ran to his store and passed out guns as long as they lasted. A.R. Mancing, another hardware dealer, grabbed a breech-loading rifle, while other citizens armed themselves with rocks.

At this show of strength, the hooligans outside yelled to their confederates inside the bank to escape.

Clel Miller was killed in the bombardment. Bob Younger's horse was slain, but he made a getaway on the same horse as his brother Cole. The outlaws galloped out of town, leaving Stiles to fend for himself.

A posse, soon numbering a thousand or more, tore after the culprits. The Younger brothers and Pitts were rounded up in Madelia, where Pitts was killed and the other surrendered. They were taken, under heavy guard, to Faribault, and later sentenced to life imprisonment. Bob Younger died there on September 6, 1889.

A special act of legislature, providing that life convicts be released after 35 years good behavior, paroled the last two Younger brothers on July 14, 1901.

James committed suicide in the St. Paul Hotel, and Cole headed for Missouri, where he ran a Wild West show with Frank James until Cole's death in 1915.

The Northfield Bank Robbery

The posse was never successful in capturing the James Brothers, who made their way to Missouri, stealing horses by day and riding at night.

The fierce, famous battle in Northfield lasted but seven minutes. When the dust settled, dead men and horses lined the streets in one of the most spectacular gun fights in history.

The loot taken from the bank amounted to a petty $290. But, the folks in Mankato lost out on a century of free advertising.

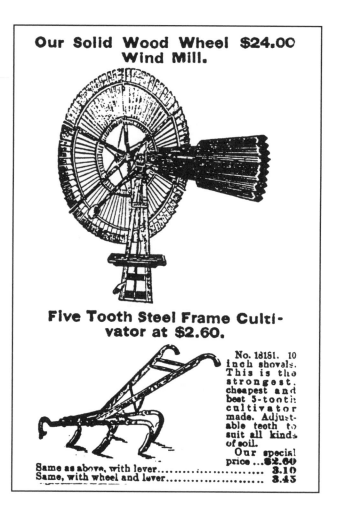

Bare essentials for man and beast at Pembina

When Pembina was little and before Grand Forks, Fargo, and Moorhead were born, George B. Winship strayed from the south via Abercrombie while Billie Budge came from Scotland by way of Abercrombie. Winship and Budge met at Pembina in 1871, where George was a store clerk. After some discussion, they decided to form a partnership and enter into business.

They selected as the ideal spot a point on the stage line between Grand Forks and Pembina known as Turtle River, where they erected a cabin. After building their cabin, the only human habitation in 1871 between Grand Forks and Pembina, they managed to stock it with the bare essentials for man and beast and opened a hotel. Old timers credited them with having an excellent stopping place, one of the best on the line.

After building their establishment, they were unable to agree on a name for it. Finally, they chose to put "Winship Hotel" facing those coming from the south, and "Budge's Tavern" on the other side to greet the ones coming from the north. While it seemed they agreed on very little, they both liked the sign over their fireplace that read "We are NOT here for our helth!". Budge was an expert turner of flap jacks, for which he charged one dollar each. Whenever a diner complained about the price he told them to go fill up on meadow hay. Both partners insisted that any supplies be paid before being consumed. However, it is said that each warned travelers not to pay the other, which too often culminated in neither one getting paid!

Both insisted in being "first", so each night they made a joint division of cash and labor. They made a calendar with who was to make fires, empty ashes or empty spittoons and pasted it to the foot of their bed. One morning Budge mistakenly built a roaring fire on a day it was thirty below, and jumped back into bed for more sleep. The frail chimney of sticks and mud, surmounted on a barrel, caught fire. Smelling smoke, Winship poked Budge in the ribs, saying "Get up! Smells like there's a fire an' it's your turn to get up."

"It ain't my turn to get up," said Budge, "I made a mistake, so YOU get up."

"Mistake or not, since you built it, it's your fire so you put it out. It's gettin' hot in here!"

The flames leaped higher until the shanty was ablaze. Winship and Budge escaped by putting a blanket over their heads. On their way out they grabbed a side of bacon, all that was saved.

They both went to Grand Forks and entered different lines of business, then finally both accepted government appointments, rather enviable names for themselves. Winship established the Grand Forks Herald, which represented the Grand Forks District in the State Senate for several terms. Budge was a member of the constitutional convention and also represented his district in the State Senate several times. He was a leader in establishing the State University and became post master of Grand Forks.

Perhaps it can be assumed that "little Pembina", along with George Winship and Billy Budge, gained maturity about the same time.

No hogs in my heaven!

Any woman who things she's smart enough to chase hogs is either a bride or plain dumb. A woman just isn't built for chasing hogs, take it from an ex-hog-chaser.

During the years of being a farmer's wife, I learned to recognize some signs that preceded moving hogs, sure as tadpoles come from frogs. For instance, if hubby made grim efforts to appear cheerful before breakfast, I knew there were hogs to be moved. A peck on the cheek and a comradely spank meant they all had to be moved. Instead of heading out to the door for the barn like his shirt-tail was on fire, he'd hang around. Then, "Got a little time?" he'd ask, rolling a wary eye. Whether I'd planned on doing it or not, I'd mention rolls to be mixed up, milker-stuff to be washed, maybe even washing the car. "This'll only take a few minutes," he'd wheedle.

Sure enough, being weak on the top floor I'd soon find myself in jeans, flapping overshoes, and gloves. I'd trudge Indian-fashion, ten steps behind him toward the hog pens, trying with scant success to look only half as ornery as I felt.

He clambers over a plank fence ahead of me, saying, "We'll put that bunch in that door,"...nodding toward three pens and four hog house doors. "You let 'em out."

Not wanting to appear too stupid, I start toward the gate of the pen he's looking at. "Not those!" he yells. "I want the batch that farrowed the last of March."

Walking slowly, I scrutinize the row of too-human eyes peering at me from between the planks. I'm trying to divide the hogs farrowed the last of March from those farrowed March first. After two starts, I open the only pen left.

Now the fun begins.

The hogs in front of the gate won't budge; then, as if at a signal, they pour through the gate, all thirty-five at once, heading in all directions. "Head 'em off!" he yells. Which bunch, I wonder, because now they've split.

He goes at a fast sprint after one bunch while I throw back my head, clench my fists and, knees high, give chase to the others. I'm still in pretty good shape, I tell myself, wishing a neighbor would drive by. I get my pigs turned around and, trying not to wheeze, trot back to The Man. Do I rate maybe a pat on the head like he gives Skipper when she brings home the cows? Not so. "You chased the only ones headed in the right direction," he says glumly.

Instant blindness sets in among the hogs. They can't see the right door, or even the hog house. Suddenly one starts at a determined run, head down, toward the gate she just left. "Stop 'er! If she goes they all will," I hear from over my left shoulder. Pig and I clash at the gate. Pound for pound, we are about the same weight; but except for an irritated grunt the sow doesn't know she hit anything. I'm sitting in the hog mire with a tramped-on foot and blood running down one leg.

Eyeing my adversary from her own level, I holler, "To heck with these stinkers!" Husband reminds, "It was stinkin' hogs like these that paid for your walk-in linen closet. Now you grab a board and whack 'er a good one!"

The sow, who has backed into a corner, glares at me balefully. I grab a board (with, oh, joy, a nail in it!) and I sock it to her. "Not there," he wails, "You'll damage the pork an' we'll get docked!" Damage the pork? The very idea makes my eyes light up for the first time since I left

the house. I'd like to embroider her ham with a rivet gun.

The sow decides I need more exercise, and she's had time for a short rest, so she shoots past me out of the gate as if jet-propelled. Husband, with the aid of snow fencing, has corralled the other thirty-four hogs at the right door and, obviously, he can't leave them. So, giving full throttle, I start chasing the runaway. After twenty feet she stops, turns, walks sedately to the hoghouse and into the right door...

Smelling more like those hogs than their own mothers do, I limp toward the house, the Medi-quick, a shower and change of clothes.

"Thanks, Ma...that wasn't so bad, was it?" Husband throws a smelly arm over my smelly shoulder.

If I remember right, he didn't get fresh rolls for dinner, or the car washed, which actually I hadn't planned to do anyhow until he'd mentioned "hogs".

Now I take great pleasure in eating a pork chop because I know it means one less hog for some poor farmer's wife to chase. Hopefully, since my pig-chasin' days, they've invented some easier, less stressful way of handling a bunch of hogs. More than likely, there's one wing of the Pentagon devoted to solving that very situation.

I am aware that, for our earthly consumption and profit, hogs are a necessary evil.

However, when I ultimately cross the Great Divide, there hadn't better be a pig in sight.

There will be no hogs in my little patch of real estate in heaven!

Red River Trail pioneers lived with danger – even mayhem!
First person accounts

Just as activity seems to congregate and take root along the highways of today, so did settlers of more than a century ago find themselves juggled toward land along one of the trails, common denominators of Minnesota, and the two Dakotas. The cloven hooves of thousands of oxen dug ruts so deep and narrow that any unfortunate beast who lost its footing, also often suffered a broken leg. Today, instead of snapping off wheels, mammoth semis butcher asphalt a foot thick beneath their wheels in record time. Either way, it was the Wadsworth, the Red River, and the Crow Wing trails that pointed the way, making migration possible.

Vast tracts of virgin fields and forests accommodated the immigrants. For want of a better word, they were called "territories", a term that sufficed long before states were born and stepped off into counties. The few towns or cities on board then, for the most part, either no longer exist or have been renamed. And so, alas, have the trails disappeared, slipping quite without notice into oblivion or become invisible parts of interstate highways. This is why each snippet of information about the trails, their carts, the stalwart men who drove the oxen, no matter which areas of these three states it comes from, must be kept and treasured.

Therefore, what with the shifting of names and places, only the stories of the brave people who lived then remain a constant, as much the truth today as they were then. By the same token, those of us who have had the mighty privilege of cleaving a small slice from civilization as we know it, to be reconstituted more than a hundred years from now by grandchildren who for us have neither names or faces, have only that, our stories, to leave them.

In view of this truth, what could be better than reading the stories of those who have gone before us?

Mrs. Rufus Farnham, 1850

I moved to the farm sixty-five years ago. The Red River carts used to pass along between my home and the river, but I was always holding a baby under an arm and drawing water from the well, so could not tell which way they went. I only saw them when they were straight in front of me. Women in those days never had time to look at anything but work.

Sugar came in a large cone. It was cracked off when needed. When purchased, a blue paper was wrapped around it. This, when boiled, made a dye of a lovely lavender shade. It was used to dye all delicate fabrics, like fringe or silk crepe. I have a silk shawl which I dyed in this way in '56 that still retains its color. Later I paid fifty cents for three teacups of sugar. This just filled a sugar bowl.

My mother used to live on First Street North. Once when I was spending the day with her, a dog sled from Fort Garry, now Winnipeg, passed the house. There were never many of these after we came for it seemed that the Red River carts had taken their places. There were six dogs to this team. They laid down and hollered just in front of the house. I suppose they were all tired out. The half-breed driver took his long rawhide whip and gave them a few cracks and they got up and went whimpering on to St. Paul. When they were rested, they would come back from St. Paul, like the wind. It only took a few days for them to come and go, to and from the fort, while it took the carts many weeks. The drivers would have suits of

skin with the hair inside. They never forgot a bright colored sash. A bridal couple came with a dog team once, after I moved here, but the sled I saw only had a load of fine furs.

I made sour emptyings bread. Very few could make it. I stirred flour, sugar and water together until it was a little thicker than milk, then set it aside to sour. When it was thoroughly sour, I put in my saleratus, shortening and flour enough to make it stiff. It took judgment to make this bread, but everyone thought there was nothing like it.

Late type Red River Cart, taken in the Fifties.
Earlier carts had tires eight inches wide.

Captain John Van der Horck, 1850

I always relied on an Indian just as I did on a white man and never found my confidence misplaced. I often went hunting with them on the sloughs out of St. Paul. Game was very plentiful. My Indian companion and I would both have a gun. He would paddle the frail canoe. We would see the game. "Bang!" would go my gun. "Bang!" would go his. I would be loading while he was shooting. All game was plenty, plenty.

Well I remember the woodcock, long bill, big, big eyes – look at you so trustingly I never could shoot them.

There were such mighty flocks of ducks and geese in season that their flight would sound like a train of cars does now. Once I went deer hunting and saw six does. They turned their beautiful faces towards me and showed no fear. I could not shoot them.

I have seen strings of those Red River carts and many, many in a string, loaded with furs coming from Fort Garry or Pembina.

Mrs. James Pratt, 1850

My father moved to Minnesota Territory in '50. We lived with my uncle, Mr. Tuttle, who had a mill for some time on this side. He was living in a small house belonging to the government, but my father and he added two

more rooms so we could stay with them. In the spring my father took up land and built a house down by the river not far from the Minnehaha Falls. He began to work on the Godfrey mill at Minnehaha. My mother was very timid. The sight of an Indian would nearly throw her into a fit. You can imagine that she was having fits most of the time for they were always around. Timber wolves, too, were always skulking around and following the men, but I never knew them to hurt anyone. Father said it used to make even him nervous to have them keep so near him. They would be right close up to him, as close as a dog would be. He always took a lively gait and kept it all the time. One night father was a little late and mother had seen more terrifying things than usual during the day, so she was just about ready to fly. She always hated whippoorwills, for she said they were such lonesome feeling things. This night she stood peering out, listening intently. Then she, who had tried so hard to be brave, broke into wild lamentations, saying, she knew the wolves or Indians had killed father and she would never see him again. My grandmother tried to calm her, but she would not be comforted until father came, then he had a great time getting her settled down. She said the whippoorwills seemed to say as she looked out in the blackness of the night, "Oh, he's killed – Oh, he's killed." What these timid

town bred women, used to all the comforts of civilization, suffered as pioneers, can never be fully understood. After that, whenever father was late, little as I was, and I was only four, I knew what mother was going through and would always sit close to her and pat her.

Our home only had a shake roof and during a rain it leaked in showers. My little sister was born just at this time during an awful storm. We thought it would kill mother, but it did not seem to hurt her.

The Indians used to come and demand meat. All we had was bacon. We gave them all we had but, when they ate it all up, they demanded more. We were much frightened, but they did not hurt us. Father used to tap the maple trees, but we could not get any sap for the Indians drank it all. That winter we lived a week on nothing but potatoes.

Our nearest neighbor was Mrs. Wass. She had two little girls about our ages. They had come from Ohio. We used to love to go there to play and often did so. Once when I was four, her little girls had green and white gingham dresses. I thought them the prettiest things I had ever seen and probably they were, for we had little. When mother undressed me that night, two little green and white scraps of cloth fell out of the front of my little low necked dress. Mother asked at once if Mrs. Wass gave them to me and I had to answer, "No." "Then," she said, "in the morning you will have to take them back and tell Mrs. Wass you took them." I just hated to and cried and cried. In the morning, the first thing, she took me by the hand and led me to the edge of their plowed field and made me go on alone. When I got there, Mrs. Wass came out to meet me. I said, "I've come to bring these." She took me up in her arms and said, "You dear child, you are welcome to them." But my mother would not let me have them. I never took anything again.

We had a Newfoundland dog by the name of Sancho, a most affectionate, faithful beast. A neighbor who had a lonely cabin borrowed him to stay with his wife while he was away. Someone shot him for a black bear. No person was ever lamented more.

In '54 my father built the first furniture factory in

Minnetonka Mills. Our house was near it. The trail leading from Anoka and Shakopee went right by the house and it seemed that the Indians were always on it. There were no locks on the doors and if there were, it would only have made the Indians ugly to use them. Late one afternoon, we saw a big war party of Sioux coming. They had been in a scrimmage with the Chippewas and had their wounded with them and many gory scalps, too. We ran shrieking for the house but only our timid mother and grandmother were there. The Sioux camped just above the house, and at night had their war dance. I was only seven years old at the time, but I shall never forget the awful sight of those dripping scalps and those hollering, whooping fiends, as they danced. I think they must have been surprised in camp by the Chippewas for they had wounded squaws, too, with them. One old one was shot through the mouth. The men were hideously painted. One side of one's face would be yellow and the other green. It seemed no two were exactly alike.

One Sunday morning I was barefoot, playing in the yard. There were bushes around and I heard a queer noise like peas rattling in a box. I could not see what made it, so finally ran in and told father. He came and lifted up a wide board over two stones. He jumped back and called to me to run in the house, then grabbed an ax and cut the head off a huge rattlesnake. It had ten rattles. We never saw its mate.

The first school taught in Minneapolis proper was taught by Clara Tuttle, a niece of Calvin Tuttle, in one of the rooms of the government log cabin where we were living in '51. The pupils were her cousins. Miss Tuttle returned to the east the next summer and died of consumption. My cousin Luella Tuttle, the next year used to go over to St. Anthony to school, on the logs, jumping from one to the other, rather than wait for the ferry.

In '58 we returned to Minneapolis to live. Old Dr. Ames was our doctor. He was one of the finest men that ever lived. I had terrible nose bleeds. His treatment was to whittle pine plugs and insert them in the nostrils. It always cured. No matter how poor a patient was, Dr. Ames always did his best. No child was ever afraid of him.

The petrified man of Marshall County!

A queer customer was lodged in to Grand Forks county jail in the summer of 1896. He was in jail, but he had never been arrested. Had never taken anything that didn't belong to him. Had never harmed even a hair on anyone's head. He belonged to someone, surely, but to whom? He was simply put in a cell for storage, sort of. He was booked, without having done anything bad and did not even have a known name.

All this came about because he was the only petrified man in Marshall County, Minnesota, or anywhere else in the world as far as anyone knew. He was toted everywhere, named in lawsuits, not to mention hours of speculation and surmise. Some thought he was manufactured, a fake.

Fifteen miles northwest of Warren, Minnesota, lies Bloomer, where this quiet specimen was discovered. An account of the find as published in the *Minneapolis Journal*, June 13, 1896, reads:

"D.M. Williams of Warren and Richard Omand on June 8 found the body of a petrified man in the town of Bloomer. The men were engaged in digging a culvert on the public highway when they made the find, about two and a half feet below the surface, in a bed of alkali clay. A large number of persons living in the vicinity saw the body exhumed and can bear witness to the genuineness of the find.

"Nature has in a wonderful manner preserved the form and feature of this man in a far more perfect condition than in any Egyptian mummy embalmed by the hands of man. Teeth, finger nails, moustache and even the color and texture of the skin show plainly. It is a splendid specimen of a man five feet, nine inches tall, muscular and well proportioned. A long hole in the chest might indicate that he had been killed, and the position of the hands and arms, the left resting on the chest and the right stretched out along the side, the hand resting on the thigh, would show that he had received a careful burial.

"As yet no one who has sufficient knowledge of anthropology to tell what race or age he belongs has examined the man. Certain it is from many proofs that the body has been in the ground at least 150 to 200 years, and possibly far longer. Possibly the body is that of a French voyager or courier dubois of the seventeenth century or it may be that of a member of some prehistoric race, whose relics and traces are occasionally seen in various parts of the state. He was certainly not an Indian."

However, there is room for doubt. The Crookster made his petrified man too perfect, too detailed. Indeed, if the relic is real, he has been busy! Has had no rest as he is exhibited from town to town. Even landed in lawsuits. At last the Grand Forks county jail gave him space until his future can be decided. It is agreed that the men who found the man did not place him in the ditch or have a part in it. Richard Omand who rented the farm on which the relic was found, sold his half interest in the creature to William Lee, then to D.M. Williams who sold it to one Peter Bergo for $175. It was then taken to Crookston and placed in a rented store building and admission was charged. The final sale of the freak was for one thousand dollars.

George H. McPherin, of Minot, North Dakota, owned the land on which the body was found. He was, to put it mildly, far from pleased. He wanted possession of the body. All of this sudden interest spooked the sheriff so that he stationed an armed guard over the relic twenty-four hours a day to insure its safety. Finally, he put him in the Crookston jail. Now arose the questions...was the body real estate or personal property. A fierce verbal battle, without precedence to turn to, ensued.

The journey for the petrified man was far from over. His rest had truly been disturbed. Anne Marie Holms, George McPherin, and M. Graham thrust the body in the limelight in Grand Forks. It was now viewed as a money-earning asset. Claims on it came from all over.

Next on the scene came two brothers, Antoine LaCount of Medicine Lake and Malve LaCount of Red Lake Falls. They went to Crookston to file a complaint against the folks in Grand Forks. They claimed it to be without doubt their very own father! They themselves had buried him, they said, in a shallow grave on that spot after being killed near Snake River in Marshall County a half-century ago.

The Crookston people admitted seeing a resemblance between the brothers and the dead man. Even two old squaws said it was, indeed, the boys' father. It was told that the father was a dealer in horses, had one leg hurt and limped. The Grand Forks claimants were arrested. Taking no chance, the Grand Forks sheriff kept the petrified man in his jail, the quietest one of the convicts therein.

The plasterer's luck in Crookston had run out. The molds used to make the "petrified" man were found. The value of the man suffered considerably. He was presumably returned to the ditch, or close to it, from whence he came.

Gout is another extremely painful form of arthritis that affects nearly two million Americans, mostly men. It occurs when the body stores too much uric acid and usually affects the large joint of the big toe. Famous throughout history, gout affected Achilles, Alexander the Great, Leonardo da Vinci, Henry VIII, Sir Isaac Newton, Charles Darwin and Benjamin Franklin along with millions of anonymous sufferers.

EASING PAIN—As Ben Franklin learned, some treatments may relieve gout and other arthritic pain, but no cure has been found.

A childhood memory anyone could envy

In Grandpa's pasture a trough lay at a right angle with the fence and on into a meadow. A hole eight or ten feet deep with three feet of water in it was used to water his nine cows after the creek ran dry during the heat of the summer. A battered pail tied to a rope with frayed ends lay nearby.

It was a privilege to be asked to water the cows. I was eight. I can still smell the wild mint, alyssum and sweet meadow grasses. It took all of my attention to coax a little water into the pail. It either turned upside down or floated. When the cows saw me they came running. They were a motley crew by today's standards. The trough I had so laboriously managed to get half full soon emptied as cows crowded around, taking long slurps. They got ahead of me.

"Now look what you've done! And you sound more like old pigs than cows," I scolded.

Finally sated, they slowed down and I gained a few inches. A loud scraping sound brought me to my knees. Shading my eyes with my hands, I peered into the dark hole.

It was dry. Grandpa's well was dry! This was awful. A catastrophe. The creek was dry and now the well, too. How long could a cow live without water?

Heels flying, I ran down the lane, jumping cowpies and thistles. I had to find Grandpa. I was sure he did not know that the lives of his herd were at stake. I found Grandpa resting at the foot of a big red oak. He saw me coming and made room for me on his lap. His shirt always smelled a little of yesterday's sweat, but I don't recall minding one bit.

"Now what brings this on?" he asked.

"Your-your cows are going to die!" I puffed. "The well is dry. How long can a cow live without water?"

"So that's the way it is, 'tis it?" he replied, holding me close.

I tried again. "Honestly, Grandpa. I can see the rocks on the bottom. The well is dry," I emphasized.

"Tell me, did the cows get their fill for today?"

Grudgingly, I nodded. Why didn't he, the very smartest man in all the world, understand? I felt sorry for him and the poor cows.

"I believe you. I really do. But let's give our old well another chance. You and I will take another look first thing in the morning."

The next morning we went down the lane. We didn't talk much. I so dreaded the minute that that dry well would erase the look of contentment from Grandpa's face. Admiring a patch of Canadian thistles in full bloom, he said, "Ah, but didn't God present us ungrateful humans with a glorious world!" Even so, I knew he'd come back with a scythe to cut the thistles after they had had their say. He allowed everything and everybody that right.

Another few minutes and we were there. The trough was dry as a bone. He swung me over the fence and we dropped to our knees beside the well.

The water in the well was as high as yesterday's highest level.

I gasped. "It *was* dry. Honestly, Grandpa!" I wailed.

"Of course it was. You weren't fibbing. I know you thought you were right. That's why we came back: to prove our old well only needed time to replenish itself."

Sticking a blade of june grass in his mouth, he went on: "You know, people are a lot like this old well. Everyone fails to meet the mark at one time or another. Don't judge too hastily. You'll meet many that just need more time to another chance to straighten their lives out. And so will you." He tousled my hair.

Today, I am making use of the concepts Grandpa swore by. If we are to succeed we have to have more than one chance to achieve health, happiness and serenity.

The crazy medical concoctions of Dakota old-timers!

Yes, yes, why not? The hard working people of Minnesota as well as North and South Dakota saw nothing wrong with having a little extra time being added to their sunset years. It was during the early 1920s that a certain Dr. R.V. Pierce showed them the way. Understandably, they jumped at it!

Concoctions such as Dr. Pierce's "Golden Medical Discovery" and his "Favorite Prescription", coming to life in his "Chemist Department" in Buffalo, New York, soon found themselves taking up prime space in apothecaries around the nation. While sales were supposedly skyrocketing, the sale of plots in graveyards failed to drop off.

What more can be said?

The illustration below represents the immense six-story building which is occupied exclusively for the manufacture of Dr. Pierce's Standard Medicines, and known as the World's Dispensary. Within its walls is prepared a series of remedies of such exceeding merit that they have acquired a world-wide reputation and sale.

World's Dispensary, 654 to 658 Washington St., Buffalo, NY.

Chemists' Department – Invalids' Hotel. Use of
microscope in the analysis of urine.

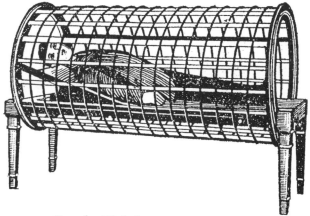

*Cage for High-frequency Treatment at
Invalids' Hotel.*

An enclosed wagon
gaudily painted to
advertise contents
sworn to cure
everything from an
ingrown toenail to
curvature of the
spine comman-
deered by a master
salesman plied
settlements several
times each year or as
long as the money
held out.

Thanksgiving story

The days before Thanksgiving at Grandpa and Grandma's house were always hectic, even when everything was planned, baked, and set. It was wild. We youngsters loved it (my mom was one of the kids).

Grandpa mostly stood around, sniffing whatever was cooking and making sure the old Majestic didn't run out of good wood. Kids kept the woodbox filled as well as the waterpail...then tried to stay out of the cook's way.

That's how it usually went...until the summer of 1919. The war was just over and Grandma wanted to show their returning soldier a real Thanksgiving dinner to sort of make up for all those K-rations he'd survived the last four years.

The folks' farm was covered with stones. As rocky as all get-out, but between those rocks was good black dirt that could raise anything; enough feed for what they needed and more. Grandma was even able to raise of a couple of dozen Minnesota Bronz turkeys. The big kind. Gobblers had tail-feather fans three feet wide. Early in September Grandma started pushing corn to them and clipped one wing so they couldn't fly over the fence, run around, and lose weight.

Choosing the exact right bird took time. They finally agreed that one big fellow would do. Actually, a dozen qualified. In the timberland grew all kinds of wild fruits, besides the half-acre of orchard. There was always so many people managed to get their knees under Grandma's table she canned mostly in two-quart jars. She could count on the Methodist preacher, his wife and seven kids, along with a snag of other relatives for sure.

The special raspberry jello mold was set the morning before the big day so it would be good and firm (no refrigeration!). That afternoon the selected bird had its head chopped off, and was cleaned and cooled down with cold water. After it was stuffed with raisin and hazelnut dressing and long before daylight the next morning it was popped into the oven for a long spell of slow roasting.

Grandma was up with the sparrows to get the jello going. The first big jar of raspberries she opened didn't look right. Didn't smell just right, either. She sent Grandpa down to the cellar to bring up another one, which passed judgment. Grandpa, trying to be helpful, took the first jar out of her way.

It was about halfway through the afternoon that one of the kids banged into the kitchen, round eyed. "Grandma, you gotta big dead turkey down in the pen."

"Can't be! They was all fine last night when I fed 'em." Everybody knows you don't feed a bird the day you butcher it.

"An' there's another one goin' down. I bet it's dead by now, too," Jim, the oldest grandchild observed. "Some of the rest don't look too healthy, neither."

Grandpa and Grandma flew to see for themselves. Sure as daylight, the kids were right. One turk knocked itself out running smack into a tree. About then a hen tumbled from a limb with a squawk, almost landing on Grandpa.

Grandma mumbled, "Well, I never..." before tears filled her eyes. The ham wouldn't fill everybody, and besides, she was known for her roast turkey and hazelnut dressing. What in tarnation was a body to do? "Kill that one in the corner quick, Grandma, before it dies," a grandchild suggested.

"Hush! Can't feed sick birds to anybody!" Grandma chided.

The kitchen door slammed. Joe, the returning soldier joined them. Hands shoved deep in pockets against the November chill he leaned over the fence. Swallowing her

tears, Grandma explained the mystery...and, whatever was she to do now?

Joe rolled the turk at his feet over with the toe of a boot. It opened one eye halfway and made a squawk that sounded like neither bird or beast. "Hell's Bells, if this was at camp, I'd say they had one last whale of a party last night. They're all dead drunk! Why'd you start feedin' stuff like that around here after I left?" Joe teased. He knew his folks were such strict teetotalers they hardly took cough syrup. Then, he started laughing until his knees buckled. When he could talk, he said, "Mom...shame on you! Gettin' poor innocent turkeys drunk." Grandpa tried to keep from smilin'.

Arms akimbo, Grandma fixed a level eye on Grandpa. "Ed, what'd you do with them raspberries you throwed out this morning?"

Grandpa shoved back his cap. He scratched his bald spot. "Well, durn it, I-I, well, you know how I hate to waste anything! I poured it in the turkeys' trough. They was crazy about it."

The kids joined Joe in having hysterics, rolling on the ground and holding their stomachs.

Dead serious, Grandma said, "Go ahead! Laugh yourselves sick. T'ain't none of you that's gotta feed the preacher drunk turkey. Do-do you 'spose it'll taste in the meat?"

Throwing an arm across her shoulders, Joe gasped, "No, Ma, don't worry. It won't taste. Put 'im outta his misery and get him in the oven. Never expected to run into booze on this place! A war sure changes people. Bet the preacher will take three pieces long as he don't know what happened."

Grandpa grabbed a gobbler and headed for the choppin' block.

Grandma turned on the kids. "First one of you rascals ever peeps I served a-a drunk turkey for Thanksgiving is going to be in real trouble! Now, you, promise an' don't you dare tell! Not ever!"

There was one last off-key gobble before the axe descended.

Instead of climbing on the wagon...that was one drunk turkey that landed on a platter.

Bonanza farms sprung up during incomparable era

Windows can be pried open and locks are made to be picked, or so it seemed to the owners of the many bonanza farms who tried to keep randy men from getting into the bunk houses of female help. Guards were posted at the kitchens and laundries where the ladies worked. None of this kept bonanza spreads from becoming a big chunk of history destined to last.

Bonanza farms ranged the length and breadth of the Red River Valley, with an average of 7,000 acres each. Many were much larger. The John Dalrymple, Sr. farm was one of the largest with a veritable army of 1,000 men employed during the peak operation season. He farmed 30,000 acres of wheat with 800 horses and mules, keeping 30 steam engines busy. Wages ran a dollar per man a day, from which fifty cents was deducted for board.

The Dwight farm, as an example, operated its own butcher shop, grocery and clothing store combination to secure supplies for the operation at a reduced cost that enabled its employees to make purchases. The Keystone Farm put up ninety tons of ice. A few of the many prominent operations were Powers, Downing, Dalrymple, Hill, Chaffee, Dwight, Grandin, Keystone and Askegaard.

Regulations on the farms were pretty much the same. A hand-written notice tacked to the bunk house wall read that "bringing or using liquor on the farm is positively forbidden, men who work require rest so lights out at 9 o'clock except on Saturday, when they may stay up on 'till 10. No firearms to be used. Dancing or scuffling must be done outside the bunk house. Clean speech and habits required at all times. Take complaints or fault finding to the one who hired you." In some spreads, such as the Keystone Farm, men were fired for talking at the table, it was rumored. For recreation, some of the men played penny ante.

Thomas Radcliff, a boss around the farm at Helendale, reported that almost everybody around had, at some time,

**Straw burning engine around 1904. Thresher requiring bandcutters.
Straw elevator with swinging stacker attachment.**

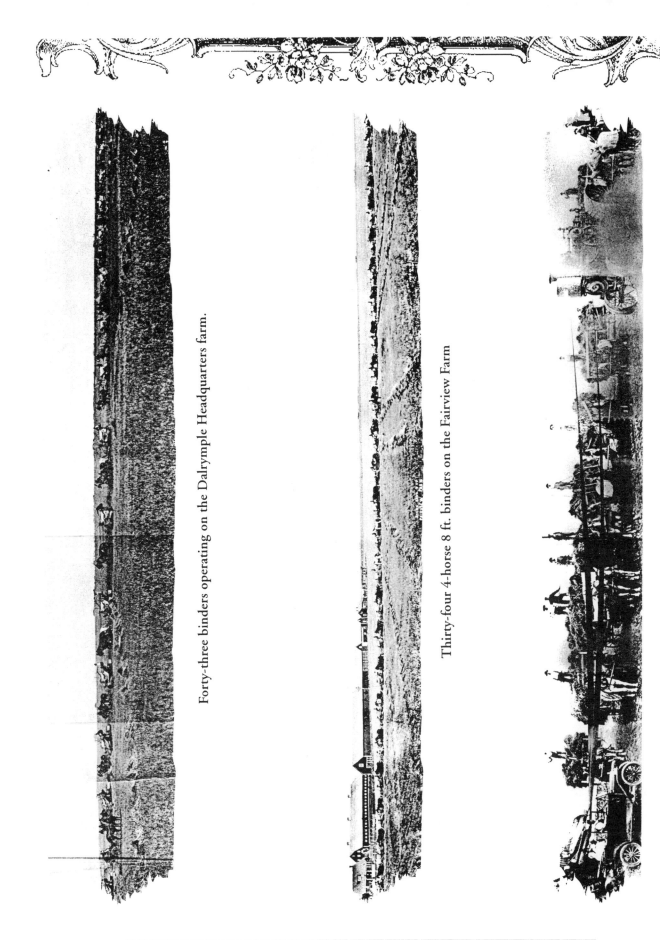

Forty-three binders operating on the Dalrymple Headquarters farm.

Thirty-four 4-horse 8 ft. binders on the Fairview Farm

Threshing scene in Richland County

worked for the Powers family. Help was almost impossible to procure for harvest. Dwight Farms were forced to hire their entire crew from green Easterners who had never seen a binder or driven a horse. One time the entire crew got into some kind of big jamboree and disappeared. This was not an uncommon occurrence.

At each harvest a "binder boss" drove a horse and buggy to be on hand when a binder ran out of twine and had to be rethreaded or needed simple repairs. He kept sharp eye out for any horse getting too tired or too hot and ordered them to the side to rest or a fresh one brought up. Any operator having a binder problem signaled for help by raising his hat into the air on the end of a long pole supplied for that purpose. One binder boss was in charge of 28 binders on the Keystone Farms and 35 binders at Fairview Farms. With so many city dudes on the equipment, it was an order that none of the machinery operators could carry a wrench or pliers.

H.F. Chaffee was one of the first owners to add livestock to his enterprise. They were an extra income and made use of what would have otherwise gone to waste. Beef and pork joined what had been just crops first and

were naturals for cleaning up a field while they got fat. It was a real boon when sheep were added to turn elevator screenings, thus far considered a waste product, into folding money. Sheep thrived on them as well as providing another cash crop with wool. Chaffee kept a flock of 14,800.

Conflict between owners was rather par with so much competition for space and men. Probably one of the best known rhubarbs was between J.B. Powell and Oliver Dalrymple, both men of ability and sound reputation, along with well defined stubborn streaks. A lengthy complicated dispute ensued. It seemed to be the consensus of many that Dalrymple came out on top, earning for him the name "Mr. Bonanza". He did not object to anyone's knowledge.

Since the beginning of bonanza days agriculture has always ranked high in mechanization. The bonanza spreads started with big machines and Red River Agriculture has remained highly mechanized ever since.

However, none of this changes the fact that today's locks are still being picked; windows pried open. It seems the more things change, the more some things stay the same.

Lunch time at Dalrymple farm No. 1 east of Casselton. Foreman,
Thorvald Thorson, standing second from right.

Fairview Farm. Adams home extreme left, mess house, bunk house, 125-head horse barn, and office building at extreme right.

960-acre wheat field on Fairview Farm

Threshing crew on Keystone Farm, Richland County, ND.

Jack Anderson custom threshing crew and cook house, 1915

A Pazandak farm harvest scene, 1910

Sheep herd at Helendale farm

Mr. and Mrs. E.B. Powell

Front porch of Dalrymple home in 1906. LEFT TO RIGHT: unknown, Mrs. John Pollock (Dorothy Dalrymple), John S. Dalrymple, Sr., and Mrs. Oliver Dalrymple.

Partial view of dining room, Downing farm, 1911.
Four tables with 25 places each.

Baking bread at the Downing farm, 1911

Kitchen at the Downing farm, 1911

Photo courtesy of Great Northern Railway

This postage stamp was made to commemorate the Omaha Exposition of 1898.

Presidential party with train on the Dalrymple farm, September 6, 1878.
President Hayes fourth from left holding top hat.

James J. Hill's Humbolt farm in Minnesota, 1899.

M.J. Gummers threshing crew near Mayville about 1889.

Weirdest house in America was in our own backyard!

Ghost of the Spring Valley mystery house

Imagine, if you can, a house with eight rooms downstairs, each with its own exit to the outside; a total of nineteen doors; two stairways leading to upstairs rooms because there was no connecting door, plus a pair of windows, visible from the outside, while only one appears on the inside.

Other features were three layers of flooring upstairs with worn spaces in the middle floor in one upstairs room that had no door. It could only be entered from the outside via a ladder and through a window. Tongue and groove ceiling boards tattled of a ghostly stairway that no one remembered. A chimney, shingled over by someone years ago, was found at the end of one room.

This structure actually existed from the 1850s until 1975, when it was torn down by Leo Galloway, who owned the farm.

The 172-acre farm, located four miles west of Spring Valley, was first purchased in lots by John W. Farquhar from a Frenchman on March 28, 1856. It was near the west side of Frankford, county seat of Mower County at the time. Fifteen acres were later sold in the 1860s for $100 to William Lamb and son, Charles.

No one is sure when this house of solid oak with its thick, limestone walls was built. Some of the mysteries of the old house have been explained to the satisfaction of most who live in the area.

A gang of famous outlaws lived there, hence the numerous exits for escape from roving lawmen. Worn places in the center layer of flooring under a window hid counterfeit plates or money until it could be picked up by other gang members.

Gang members were also professional horse thieves. Once on the place, horses seemed to disappear without a trace. The reason, it was said, was because they were hidden in a large cave on the property and the entrance was camouflaged.

The Galloways examined every foot of the farm but found no traces of the cave. Most likely, Emily Galloway explains, that's because the rumor – that the cave entrance was sealed with rocks many years ago – is true.

A Free Will Baptist Church, located on one corner of the farm, burned to the ground before it was a year old. It burned the night a sheriff's posse was reported on its way to look for counterfeit plates in its belfry.

Several years ago the Galloways built a new home near the old site. Do the unexplained mysteries of the place bother them? Having lived in the house from 1941 until 1975, Emily Galloway feels very much at home.

"Besides," she asks, "who could be lonely on a place peopled by so many interesting ghosts, tenanting a house that defies duplication anywhere?"

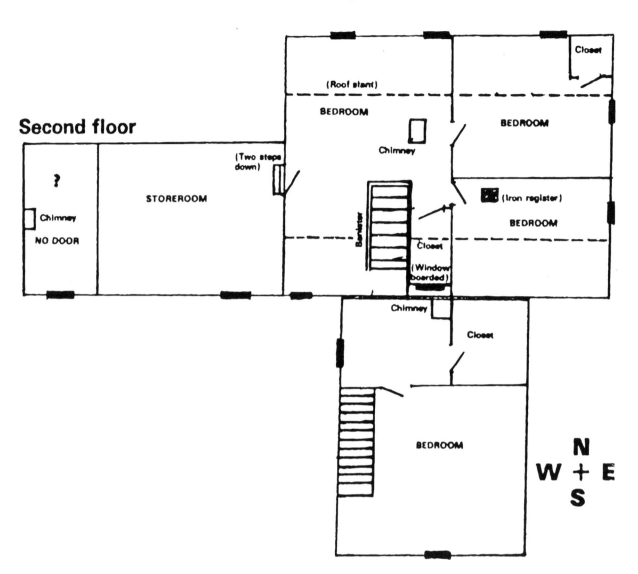

Second floor

?
Chimney
NO DOOR

STOREROOM

(Two steps down)

(Roof slant)

BEDROOM

Chimney

Banister

Closet

(Window boarded)

Chimney

Closet

BEDROOM

Closet

BEDROOM

(Iron register)

BEDROOM

N
W + E
S

Mrs. Galloway provided these floorplans of the "mysterious" home (now demolished). "The kitchen, pantry and dining room, in the northeast corner of the ground floor, were part of the original house. That portion had a basement," explains Mrs. Galloway. "The south wing, a separate house, was moved to the site and attached to the original for Grandma Lamb (mother of former owner William Lamb) during the 1800s. Upstairs rooms of this portion have no connecting door to the original house. The west wing was built on for the hired help. Cupboards were built out into the west wing, probably in the 1920's. The partition between the bedroom and the dining room of the original dwelling was taken out, and the picture window added, sometime between 1910 and 1919," says Mrs. Galloway. A particularly intriguing aspect of the house concerns the second story of the addition on the west. "The west room of the west wing had no door. The only way to get into it was from the outside through the window. "Unless one noticed." says Mrs. Galloway, that the bedroom only had one window, when two were visible from outdoors, one might not realize there was.another room. When that wing was torn down, we found three floors. The middle one was worn half through in front of that window."

Ground floor

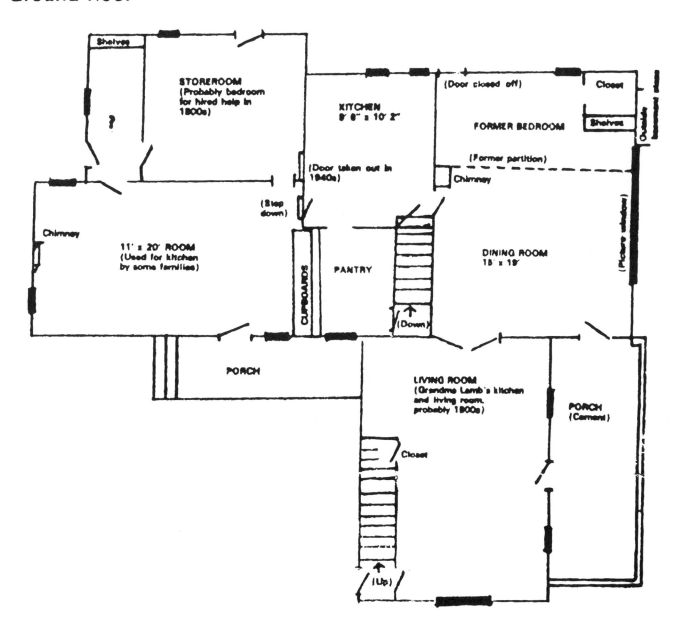

Shelves

STOREROOM
(Probably bedroom
for hired help in
1800s)

?

KITCHEN
9' 8" x 10' 2"

(Door closed off)

Closet

FORMER BEDROOM

Shelves

(Former partition)

(Door taken out in
1940s)

Chimney

(Step
down)

Chimney

11' x 20' ROOM
(Used for kitchen
by some families)

CUPBOARDS

PANTRY

DINING ROOM
18' x 18'

(Picture window)

(Down)

PORCH

LIVING ROOM
(Grandma Lamb's kitchen
and living room,
probably 1800s)

PORCH
(Cement)

Closet

(Up)

Fergus Falls Anti-Horse Thief Association planned necktie parties

Thus ran a headline in the summer of 1876 that ran in the St. Paul Pioneer Press. In addition to the "gentlemen of the road", Otter Tail County in the city of Fergus Falls harbored horse thieves. Or so they thought. Actual horse thievery was more often reported in the popular Pomme do Terre in Grant County, and on to Stevens County, the home of Jagger, their reputed "fence". Although never proved to be engaging in such an industry, Jagger was never out from under suspicion of this cruddy practice. He was ever in a cloud of smoke, even if a real fire was never detected.

Fergus Falls citizens were staunch believers in preparedness. The very word "rustlers" sent them into shock. They opted to "lock the door *before* the horse was stolen". In March, 1872, a vigilante committee was formed. They called themselves the Anti-Horse Thief Association. All this, despite the belief of some that there wasn't a horse in all of Fergus Falls valuable enough to tempt even the most indiscriminate of horse thieves. This did not deter the committee. The following is the constitution of the Anti-Horse Thief Association: *Whereas, the experience of the last year has demonstrated the necessity of some further protection from the depredations of an infamous band of horse thieves who infest the county, preying upon the property of the community, other or than that afforded by the civil laws of the state, therefore.*

Resolved, That the formation of a Vigilance Committee for our protection is imperatively demanded.

Resolved, That the name of this society shall be the Fergus Falls Anti-Horse Thief Association, and shall have for its object the recovery and protection of horses stolen from the members, and the prompt punishment of the thieves.

Extract from the by-laws:

It shall be the sworn duty of any and all members of this society capturing a horse thief having in his possession the property of any member of the association, to promptly ex-

ecute this said horse thief, by hanging, or in the absence of facilities for hanging, by shooting, or in any other manner, but in any and all events to take such effective measures as shall preclude the possibility of the return of said horse thief.

The entire town, according to the report, attested to this program, with the most visible exception of one man, the druggist. He obviously went out of his way to keep his distance, in fact, went farther than that by erecting a sign outside his store that in brazen terms ridiculed the association.

Each day the druggist changed his "bulletin board", one day ridiculing the association, commenting on its members, their courage, or lack thereof, and the manner in which the thieves were disposed of. One day he hung a rope on his bulletin board for the convenience of the association in case they caught a thief they believed was "too good to be shot". People laughed but could not help noticing how popular the place had become to every less-than-sterling character who rode into town.

Then the druggists brother-in-law came to town. The druggist and he had never met. Their common bond was both having married orphan trail girls, separated in early girlhood, who had not seen each other since. The planned two weeks stay of the newly-found relatives stretched to six weeks before they returned to their southern Minnesota home.

Not long after their return home. Fergus Falls Jacob Austin received a letter from the brother-in-law. It stated that since he considered himself a good citizen, he felt it his duty to report that he had discovered the druggist to be a bad man, directly connected to the horse thieves. No only that... but, he harbored undesirable characters in the house.

However, the charge was never made against the druggist. He left town too soon!

Run fer yore life!

On that spring day of 1871, one Solitary Passenger rattled around in the drafty old stage. The driver, name of "Pattin", drove from a seat on top, the express box that held mail and money, roped at his side. About six miles west of Otter Tail City a horse with a masked rider plunged out of the trees to stick a double barreled shotgun under the nose of Pattin. Frantically, without being told, he cut the box loose and whipped his team into a lather in his effort to get to safety.

While all of this was taking place, a Solitary Passenger dived out a side door on the opposite side of the stage into the brush, putting as much real estate under this boots as possible in the shortest length of time. The driver, not stopping for his passenger and relieved of the express box, made stellar time. On knees that had suddenly turned to rubber, in a voice that trembled with fright, he told of his harrowing experience to the first person he met. A posse was thrown together pronto and they took off in a frenzy to catch the culprit.

E.E. Corliss
Photo Courtesy of Ottertail
Historical Society

Following the track of the stage the first six miles was no problem. Then, when they came upon tracks making a hasty dash for the woods toward the north, were elated! Wheeling their horses in that direction, they soon came upon Solitary Passenger, clothes nearly torn off from the brush, half-dead with fright that turned into stricken misery when the leader of the troop affixed a rope around his neck, tied a hangman's knot, and started looking for a suitable limb.

To prove that there is honor among a posse as well as thieves, Solitary Passenger was given five minutes in which to say his final prayer. He chose to use this time, instead, to conceivably gasp, "I ain't him! I'm jest a runnin' fer my life!" A level head among the other kind in the posse prevailed, and it was decided to take solitary passenger back with them for driver Pattin to identify as the man who robbed the stage. After a long, level look, heavy with the responsibility of knowing his decision spelled whether this man lived or died, Pattin said slowly, "Y'know, I ain't sure. I never got a real good gander at the feller on my stage, an' I never did see the bandit without that rag around his mug." Instant semi-rigor mortis set in again for Solitary Passenger. The posse remained mystified. The execution was postponed until further developments.

After a few days the law was allowed to take its course.

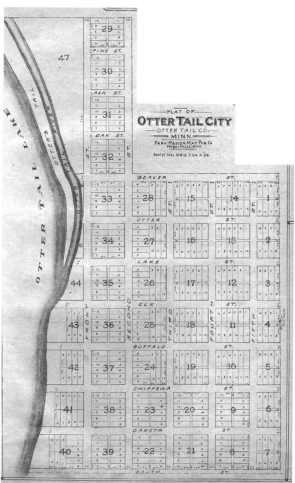

Platbook of Ottertail County Minnesota, 1902
Photo Courtesy of Ottertail Historical Society

The Minnesota Stage Company was eager to get it settled. Another likely prospect had been imprisoned along with Solitary Passenger, much to his relief. That fall, before court in Otter Tail County set, the stage company sent an agent to Otter Tail City to interview the new county attorney, E.E. Corliss, the incumbent.

The agent arrived only to find that the county attorney was out on his acreage at Clitherall. The agent knew this spot to be on the shores of a lake, he envisioned shade and something cool to drink, a place that later became known as "Camp Corliss". When the agent arrived he saw a tall red-headed man in shirt sleeves and barefoot industriously helping a stone mason, later to be identified as the county treasurer. He asked, "Do you know where I can find Mr. Corliss?"

"Yes," said the working man, "I'm Corliss."

"What! YOU are the Otter Tail County Attorney?", the agent gasped.

"Well, I should smile I am! What do you want?".

The agent looked Corliss over, then said "Well, I did want to convict a robber, but...I think I might as well let him go."

Attorney Corliss reportedly closed one eye, took his time looking the agent over with the other, then said "My friend, you just have your witnesses here and I'll do the rest."

The case was tried, the rightful robber convicted, and the agent came away with a different opinion of the new county attorney.

Attorney Corliss led a long successful life, making quite a name for himself, as one also hopes did Solitary Passenger.

A prairie fire

One of the most remarkable instances of suffering and loss by a prairie fire occurred October 18, 1876. The *Fergus Falls Journal*, in giving an account of the fire, said:

"Auden Johnson and H.P. Stevens, who resided near Wall Lake, in Dane Prairie, while on their way to Campbell station with an ox team loaded with wheat, saw a furious prairie fire coming from the southeast. They thought it quite distant, but deemed it prudent to set a back-fire. But the advancing flames came upon them so rapidly that before they succeeded in lighting a match in the wind the demon was upon them. Their frightened teams became unmanageable and ran from the fire and the men at first directed their efforts to save their teams as well as themselves. Seeing their attempts were in vain, they finally threw themselves on their faces in the grass, and the roaring mad sea of fire passed over them. It was a terrible moment.

Mr. Stevens gives a very intelligent account of the case. He says they deliberately fell on their faces, knowing it was their only hope, but for some time they abandoned all hope of their lives.

"The fire having passed, the men were in the most pitiable condition. They were badly burned all over their bodies, particularly on their hands and faces, which where a mass of blisters, while their eyes were swollen shut. In this suffering condition, they were found in the evening by a man passing with a horse team, who brought them to Fergus Falls to the homes of friends for medical attention.

"One of the teams was overtaken in high grass and prostrated by the fire and so badly burned that they will possibly die. The other team reached a point where the grass was lighter and was not so seriously burned. The wagons were more or less injured and the wheat badly damaged."

Big Bad Bill Wilson

Big Bad Bill Wilson was baaaaad! If you don't believe it, just ask him. One look was enough. Besides being one of the biggest men anybody ever saw, he sported an unruly beard, his brow was furrowed and he was cross-eyed, with a voice that sounded as if it came from beneath his size thirteen boots. Hero worship was intense on the frontier, and Big Bad Bill filled the bill. Besides, he was a merciless bully.

It sounds contradictory to say next that Big Bad Bill was also not quarrelsome....unless provoked. He never started a "rough house"...unless in the mood. He was guilty of bragging about his prowess, how mean he could be, and people believed him. They were scared not to!

It so happens that most of Big Bill's admirers were young fellows. To prove how much they wanted to be like him they often got into trouble with each other around him. One level, long look from whichever one of Bill's eyes was pointed in their direction was enough, usually, to quell anything they had in mind. Bad Bill worked in the pineries in the winter and come down into town to "rest" for the summer. One time a school meeting, where feelings ran high, was scheduled. A hot time was expected. Both sides counted Bad Bill to show up on their side.

The meeting was in a vacant store building. Among the opposition was a lawyer, Newton H. Chittenden, who became superintendent of schools for Otter Tail County. He was almost as big as Big Bad Bill. Everyone hoped that there would be a scrap. Chittenden was cold, reserved, had been a lieutenant in the army. He was not liked, much less idolized than Big Bill.

As was anticipated, things got warm at the meeting. Accusations flew, with Chittenden claiming some folks voted twice. If there ever was an invitation to bring on Big Bad Bill, this was it! He was brought from a back room. Every stinking muscle-bound pound of him worked its way slowly through the crowd, casting an evil eye here-and-there. People pulled necks far down into coat collars if he looked their direction.

Bad Bill over-estimated his prowess when he came within reach of Chittenden. One arm shot out, a muscular hand grabbed Bill's shoulder, while the other followed suit, attaching its-self to the seat of his pants. A fast rush through the crowd followed toward the nearest door. Chittendem aimed the toe of his boot at the seat of Bad Bill's behind and let fly!

Big Bad Bill picked himself up out of the middle of the street, spitting gravel. By the next morning the population of the town was down by one. Big Bad Bill Wilson was heard of no more.

When Hewitt Bank was new.

(Notice photo of Taft in window.)

Love child

James G. Craigie, a Scotch man, established a claim; he built a house and a flour mill close to the lake on a small stream. Besides himself, there was his wife and a daughter, Annie. Annie was in her late teens and a "love child", conceived in Scotland and born in one of the Dakotas. Craigie married his wife soon after they came from Scotland.

Craigie, being a true Scotsman, was thrifty. He somehow knew he would be a success when he first laid eyes on this piece of real estate. It was on the south shore of Otter Tail lake, which was about ten miles long and six miles wide. There was a clear little stream, fine heavy timber, and sandy beaches. Just what he was looking for!

The Indians loved it, too. In the early times the Sioux and Chippewas fought for possession of the favorite hunting grounds. The Chippewa finally won and held possession, thanks to their able chief, Po-Ka-no-ga, who was also a friend of the white man.....until he was made to move his people to the White Earth reservation. Indian mounds abound from the south side of the river back over the prairie, large and impossible to miss.

Annie Craigie was fair to look upon and as well schooled as possible. Her mother and father doted on their comely daughter. As it so happens, so did one Archie McArthur. He was a fine specimen of manhood, lived near them and a worker. In his veins, however, ran blood from a Scotch father.....and an Indian mother. Although his blond good looks belied this Indian connection.

Annie loved Archie and Archie loved Annie, but that was the end of it as far as her parents were concerned. They violently opposed the union, up to the point of and including the demand that if they married....they were "never to darken the door" again! As far as anyone knows, they didn't.

While this fiasco was unfolding here, a man by the name of "John Comb", a Scotsman, was working his way into this country, with his sights set on obtaining a hunk of land near Craigie. He was married, well educated, and soon found himself filling important state positions.

Also at this time, a woman near the Craigie home in Scotland came to visit her old neighbors in America. It was an item in a newspaper back in the old country that tipped her off as to the new address of John Combs, her husband. The Craigies swore by the story that she was, in deed, Comb's wife. That he deserted her so that he might come to America with another woman.

Mrs. Combs headed directly toward a lawyer little knowing that tragedy would rear its ugly head to prevent the proceedings ever being applied. It happened one sunny afternoon, with a fine breeze blowing, when Craigie, as he often did, took his sail boat out on the beautiful lake to give his wife and Mrs. Combs a ride. They were only well out on the lake when who-knows-what happened and all were drowned.

Now comes the frey!

James G. Craigie had siblings. Some of them still in Scotland, some in Canada, and one in Minnesota. Alexander H., who lived in Scotland, came to Minnesota and approached the probate court of Otter Tail County to acquire letters of administration of the estate of James G. Craigie, his dead brother.

When news of the proceedings reached the ears of Annie McArthur, she stoutly protested, crying "No way! I am the legal daughter of James Craigie!" However, Alexander Craigie was appointed administrator. Annie appealed to district court. Craigie siblings from all directions , claiming that Annie was not the child of James Craigie, but of a man by the name of "Falkner", who still lived in Scot-

land! If they could prove this, the property of a thrifty, well-to-do brother would be theirs. It was up to Annie to prove that she was the sole heir. Could she?

The trial was not only talked of in the town, but environs far beyond. Almost to a man, sympathies lay with Annie who was, in a sense, one of their own. Who did these foreigners think they were, to come steamin' in like a bunch of hornets?

All of the Craigie relatives attested to the fact that Annie was a Falkner, begotten in Scotland, not a Craigie. Also, that the reputation of her mother left much to be desired. The jury was given the instructions that if they believed from the testimony of the plaintiff that Annie was begotten in Scotland; that her mother and James lived near each other and that James followed her mother to America where she gave birth to the child, then married her two years later, the Craigie siblings would win.

The jury could not, upon lengthy deliberation, forget the letters and books Annie produced, signed "Your Affectionate Father", ever introducing her as his daughter. They announced that Annie McArthur to be, beyond the shadow of a doubt, the daughter of James G. Craigie, as decreed by the Supreme Court of Minnesota.

Scrimping money for Archie and Annie McArthur and their children was over.

Score love child, one: greedy relatives, zero!

James G. Craigie
Photo Courtesy of Ottertail Historical Society

A lynch court at Mankato

The trial of John Campbell broke all records in the annals of Minnesota. It was a weird trial. There was a judge and a jury and when the case was ended, Mr. Campbell was dangling from a rope, very dead.

Lawyers won't find the case cited in the Minnesota law books, and strictly speaking, it probably wasn't a trial at all, but it was effective enough to suit all practical purposes. Moreover, it was mercifully short, for Campbell was hauled before an impromptu court, tried, found guilty and lynched, all within about two hours. Justice certainly couldn't have been blind at Mankato in 1865, nor yet slow.

The story of the hurry-up demise of John Campbell presents few refinements, and he was no subtle or crafty criminal. His remarkable trial was the thing that today perpetuates his memory. He must have come of bad stock. One of his brothers was hanged at Mankato in 1862 as an aftermath of the Sioux Outbreak. He was a half-breed. He had served in the army only to become a deserter. Besides this he was reputed to have killed two or three Indians, before the ghastly Jewett episode.

Andrew J. Jewett was a prominent citizen of Garden City in Blue Earth County. He had been postmaster there until he bought a small farm near the village, where he lived with his young wife, a two-year-old son, his elderly parents, and a farm hand. As a consequence of a business transaction he came into the custody of five hundred dollars in cash, and in some way Campbell learned of this fact.

There were too many persons on the Jewett farm for him to attempt a raid alone, so he induced five other half-breeds to join him on an expedition to get possession of the money. He told them as an additional inducement that he was out to avenge the death of his brother.

On the morning of May 2, 1865, the Jewett family had gathered around the table for breakfast when sud-

denly the band of malevolent half-breeds appeared at a door of the small cabin. Mrs. Jewett snatched up her son and attempted to escape through another door at the opposite side of the building. She was immediately followed by her husband. The attackers opened fire, and Mrs. Jewett fell dead. Her husband was shot and then tomahawked to death. The child was left on the ground for dead. The farm hand also was killed, as were both of the older Jewetts.

After that the marauders looted the cabin, Campbell making away with the money. They traveled a short distance away from the place and calmly proceeded to cook their dinner. Having no further use for his partners in the atrocious crime, the ringleader abandoned them and started along the road for Mankato.

Early that same morning the wholesale murders at the Jewett farm were discovered by a neighbor, who spread the alarm. The child, it was found, did not die, and the only one to escape the fiends, although the older Jewett remained alive for a few hours. On the Mankato road Campbell was arrested and taken into town, where he gave a very bad account of himself. He claimed that his name was Pelky and that he knew nothing of any murder or murders, but despite his story he was clapped into jail to await further investigation. He proved himself to be a very stupid villain. In his pocket was found a woman's handkerchief that apparently belonged to one of the Jewetts, and he was wearing stockings, a coat and pants of some of his victims. It wasn't long before he was positively identified as John Campbell.

There was tremendous excitement in Blue Earth County next morning, and at an early hour eight hundred furious men had gathered in the vicinity of the Mankato jail. There was much talk of the advisability of a lynching party, while the cooler heads counselled delay. The crowd was in an ugly temper when it was proposed that Campbell be tried at once, a sort of compromise be

132

tween lynching and a regular trial. It was feared that General Sibley's soldiers might appear at any time and take the prisoner away.

It was finally decided to have the trial early in the afternoon. A certain S.F. Barney was speedily named as judge and a jury selected. The trial was conducted out in the open where the present courthouse now stands.

Campbell was brought out of jail and permitted to state his case. He insisted that he had been captured by hostile Indians who robbed him of his clothes and forced him to wear the ones he had on when taken into custody. The prosecution proved glaring errors in his statements of the two days, and the judge instructed the jury to give the murderer the benefit of all doubt.

The jury went out, deliberated for half an hour, and came in with a remarkable verdict. It said that Campbell was guilty, but recommended that he be again tried at a regular term of the district court. The crowd that had collected for revenge and a show weren't impressed by the

recommendation for a second trial. Moreover, it had already found exactly the right rope for a lynching ceremony; so some of the more reckless rushed up to the prisoner and began dragging him toward a convenient basswood tree.

For a time it appeared as though the advocates of lynching and the friends of law and order would come to blows. For ten or fifteen minutes it was a scene of wild disorder; and guns, knives and revolvers were flourished. Those in favor of hanging were more numerous, however, and it wasn't long before Campbell had said his last prayers to a priest, confessed his crime and the hiding place of the money, and was completely dead.

Later the half-breeds who had participated in the wanton murders were killed by a posse headed by a scout named "One Armed Jim".

John Campbell's trial may not have been authorized by any of the statutes of Minnesota, but it was conclusive, and it was unique.

The "Blueberry War"

Some of the Twin City papers were derisive – they were unkind. They made sport of John Gurrell, calling him "The Hero of the Blueberry War". Gurrell was the sheriff of Crow Wing County, and everyone around Brainerd said he did the best he could under the circumstances.

The genesis of the "Blueberry War" (and don't be misled, there were casualties in this war) was in the mysterious disappearance of Helen McArthur, the twenty-two-year-old daughter of a farmer who lived a few miles out of the village of Crow Wing. One day in the spring of 1872 Helen started toward town with her sister. When they were half way toward their destination, the sister decided to return to the farm. Helen did not come back that night, but there was no anxiety about her. It was believed she had decided to stay with friends in town. When several days passed and she did not return, an investigation was begun, but no trace was found of the girl, except some of her clothes on a river bank. She was never found, but there were many theories as to what misfortune had befallen her.

One rumor had it that she had eloped with a lumberman, but for a time the majority of the neighbors held to the opinion that she had committed suicide. As evidence they noted that before she had left home she had "taken off her hoops and carefully put them away". Usually she had worn a hoop skirt, which was the fashion of the day, when she went visiting. It was thought that she had been despondent over some love affair, had gone to the river, loaded down her clothes with rocks, and jumped into the stream to be drowned. Next it was reported that she had been seen in the vicinity of Leech Lake among the Pillager Indians, by whom she was said to have been kidnapped. The search was vigorously pushed in that sec-

tion, but nothing was found to indicate that she ever had been there. Inadvertently a clue was unearthed that led to much excitement and the famed "Blueberry War".

One day a passing white settler heard a suspicious conversation in the teepee of a half-breed Chippewa. The squaw of the half-breed was upbraiding her husband because he had beaten her too severely and too frequently. She threatened that if he ever did it again she would tell all she knew of his connection with the death of the McArthur girl. Immediately the settler informed the authorities of what he had heard, and the half-breed, along with a brother, was placed under arrest at Brainerd. They were charged with having attacked the girl, murdered her, and disposed of the body by tying rocks around her neck and casting her into the river. The men were arrested in July, and when they asked for time to find witnesses to prove their innocence, the court continued the case for several weeks. The people of the community had been inflamed by the alleged deed and were incensed by the action of the court in postponing the trial.

This was the situation on the night of July 23. Sheriff John Gurrell was sitting in the jail at his desk, peacefully writing out reports, when suddenly the doors of the building were unceremoniously broken down by a mob of approximately a thousand citizens of Brainerd, Crow Wing, and Little Falls. They demanded the persons of the half-breed prisoners and, when the sheriff made some show of resistance, they tied him up securely and went out on a lynching bee.

Down at the other end of the street on which the jail stood, and opposite the Last Turn Saloon, was a large pine tree that seemed to be providentially designed for stringing up culprits whose presence on earth was no longer

considered of any value, and carrying the terrified wretches with it, the mob made off in that direction. When they arrived at the spot, a rope was immediately produced by someone in the crowd and tossed over a limb of the pine tree. The victims were given an opportunity to pronounce prayers and then the hanging was begun. One of the prisoners died without a struggle, but the other succeeded in tearing his arms loose and climbing hand over hand up the rope until he was sitting astride a branch overhead. His doom, however, was delayed but a moment, for guns barked and he tumbled off, dead. The bodies were left hanging to the pine tree until morning, when they were cut down and buried by Sheriff Gurrell. The *Brainerd Tribune* concluded its report of the affair by saying "And thus ended, by a fearful scene, the lives of two half-breeds, acknowledged on all sides to be very bad Indians."

But this was not the end of the episode. The day following the lynching, the report was spread around that two hundred Chippewas were assembling, ready to charge on the town of Brainerd and destroy the population to avenge the death of the two half-breeds, one of whom, with a rope around his neck, had said that his companion had killed Helen McArthur as charged. Sheriff Gurrell then turned the trick that, according to the metropolitan papers, gave him the undisputed title of "Hero of the Blueberry War". He telegraphed Governor Austin frantically: "Please send troops immediately; town full of Indians, and have been ordered to leave, but do not."

In response to the appeal the governor dispatched three companies of the national guard, and an order was issued to the commanding officer of Fort Ripley to set out with his entire garrison, with rations for thirty days, to be on hand in case of trouble. The troops arrived on the twenty-fifth, prepared for a desperate battle and a prominent place in the history books. But they were disappointed. All the warriors who should have been daubing on war paint and dressing up their feathers were out in the bushes picking blueberries, and so the titanic struggle came to be known as the "Blueberry War".

James Root, hero
of the Hinckley fire!

The "No. 4 Limited", southbound from Duluth for St. Paul, pulled out of the station at 1:55 P.M., exactly as announced in the time tables. That first day of September, 1894, the engineer on the train was James Root of White Bear. His courage had already been proved, for he had been at the throttle of the engine that carried William T. Sherman on that historic march from Atlanta to the sea. He needed all his courage that eventful September day. Practically alone and unaided, he saved the lives of nearly four hundred persons and escaped death himself only by the narrowest margin. It was the day that a tornado of flame swept up out of the southwest, burning to ashes everything in an area of three hundred fifty square miles, sending four hundred twenty to ghastly and tragic deaths, doing a damage of $3,000,000, and completely destroying six Minnesota villages and wiping out innumerable farms and hundreds of acres of giant forests. There had been few rains that year and the entire northern portion of the state was tinder dry, an open invitation for the disaster.

"No. 4 Limited" was the crack train of the St. Paul and Duluth Railway Company and consisted of one combination car, one day coach, and two chair cars. Nothing eventful was experienced until the train was well out of Duluth, when the sky became overcast and Root found it necessary to light the lamps in his cab to watch his water glass and other instruments. Since forest fires were common in that part of the state, there was nothing alarming in the mid-afternoon darkness. For forty miles the train plunged along through total blackness, the headlight making a trail through the smoke and haze. Back in the coaches the passengers read their papers and magazines and amused themselves in other ways, entirely unconcerned.

As the train approached Hinckley Hill, about a mile and a half north of that town, the sky cleared for a moment and Root saw a swarm of people racing down the track as if from some monstrous horror. He immediately stopped his train, jumped out of his cab and learned from the first refugees that all Hinckley was a furnace, that the blistering heat carried along by a terrific wind was instantly charring everything in its path. Within a few minutes approximately three hundred persons – men, women, children, babes in arms – were packed into the coaches of the train, bringing the number on board to almost four hundred. Meantime, the intense heat had become almost unbearable and Root decided to back the train toward Skunk Lake, a small station four miles north. He waited as long as he dared, and then, as an explosion burst the window of his cab, breaking the glass into a thousand pieces and cutting a great gash on his forehead, he reversed his engine and started the perilous trip through blazing forests. As the engine started to move, two men jumped on the pilot. One soon fell off and was burned, but the second reached safety with the other passengers. By that time the fuel in the coal car had become ignited and all of the coaches were on fire.

Before the engineer had gone far, the loss of blood and the heat caused Root to faint on the floor of his engine, which continued to run unattended for about two miles, until he regained consciousness. He was alone, for his fireman had climbed into the water tank. Root's hands were so burned that he was afraid to rub them for fear of tearing off the flesh. It was inky dark outside, but he made a supreme effort, gathered the remnants of his strength, crawled outside and found the train providentially stopped on the Skunk Lake bridge. On both sides of the embankment was a swamp, covered with a few feet of water. He

managed to drag himself to it, where lay insensible for hours.

While Root was heroically making that run, there was pandemonium inside the coaches. The train had burst into flames in the short but hazardous journey through a shower of falling cinders. According to George C. Dunlap, one of the passengers, "blazing embers of all shapes and sizes were hurled upon the cars. The burning forest around us was fanned by the gale, and the heat and smoke became well-nigh unbearable. It seemed as though a huge mountain of flame were rolling upon us. The baggage car took fire and thus our destruction seemed to be made certain."

The immortal race for Skunk Lake lasted only seven minutes, although it seemed seven hours. The window glass melted, curtains vanished, and the fire swept through the cars at will. The passengers stood huddled together in the aisles, some praying, some crying, others dazed. To breathe was torture. "Once the train gave a sudden lurch and we feared the cars had left the track and that the end had come," Dunlap said. "At last we arrived at Skunk Lake, none too soon, for scarcely had the coaches been deserted when they became completely enveloped in flames and were destroyed in a few minutes."

Another passenger on the doomed train was W.H. Blades of Duluth, who adds to the description of the ride. He said it required twenty minutes to make the hazardous run and that "we had not gone far before things became extremely wild, as live fire enveloped the cars and broke the glass in the windows. Transoms commenced to crack and burst, thus letting tongues of flame through the splintered openings – I do not think the large majority realized the full horror of the situation until later. As for myself, I gave up the idea of ever coming out alive. We wet towels and cloths and passed them in to the passengers in the car. The nearest approach to a panic I came in contact with in the whole ride was when a stranger put the question to me, 'What chances do you think we have of getting out of this?' and I replied, 'About one in twenty thousand,' at which he made a dive for the platform and would have left the train, had I not pulled him back into the car the held the door on him."

But despite the appalling fierceness of the fire, James Root did bring "No. 4 Limited" back to a place of refuge and saved four hundred passengers through his bravery.

A mail order bride

Hester Crooks was a mail order bride. Not that modern ingenuity in bringing prospective husbands and wives together through the convenience of United States postmen was dreamed of in 1834, but it amounted to practically the same thing in the case of Hester. The service was not as fast then as it is now, but the results were fortunate, and it is surprising that one of the mail order matrimonial agencies has not seized on Hester's romance to promote its own business. Everything turned out well for her when she married the Reverend William Thurston Boutwell, a handsome young cleric who had come out from the Atlantic seaboard to make Christians of the heathen Indians.

But first a word about Hester and how she happened to get her husband. Her father was a fur-trader and her mother a Chippewa half-breed. She was born on Drummond Island in Lake Huron, on May 30, 1817. With her family she made the perilous trip from that island to Mackinac in the mackinaw boat, narrowly escaping disaster on the journey. She attended a mission school, and became so proficient that she became a school teacher at Yellow Lake in western Wisconsin, where she taught the young Chippewas their A.B.C.'s.

Before she left Mackinac, however, a gallant youth appeared at the house of her father. Although she was very young and they had few opportunities for becoming acquainted after he left to take charge of a mission at Leech Lake in northern Minnesota among the unruly Pillagers, she remembered him better than any other young man. He was constantly with her in her daydreams as she went about her teaching at Yellow Lake. Hester was lonesome, for personable young men were not numerous.

At Leech Lake, the earnest and sincere missionary likewise had his pleasant memories, and, while he tried to bend his difficult flock to Christian ways, his mind ran back to the little girl in the fur-trader's shack at Mackinac. However, regardless of how much he may have thought of Hester during his lonely hours, his courtship was hastened by more practical matters. He soon learned that among the Indians he would count for little until he had acquired a wife. Unless he married and established a home, they thought of him as a trader and a drifter; so they would give little heed to his teachings, for traders were not looked upon with admiration. They were a bit too sharp in their methods of dealing with their Indian customers.

So, like a good, conscientious missionary concerned over the welfare of his sheep, he sat down to consider what could best be done. He had been living with a trader's family, but had left because of the fear of the taint of commercialism. Later he wrote of how he sat down alone and struggled with his problem.

"I was willing to return alone," he said in a letter, "but experience had taught me that while I resided in a trader's family, however I might be called a missionary, it was impossible to remove the impression from the Indians' minds, that I was interested in the trade. To build me a cottage and live alone, I could not live above suspicion, from the fact that single men – are in the habit of keeping a mistress.

"In view of all those circumstances, what was my duty? In brief I must tell you, after a prayerful consideration of the subject, what I did. I cast my eye over this barren desolate land, and asked, is there a helper? Instead of going into the first lodge I should chance to fall upon and throwing down my blankets, Providence directed me to send a dispatch, three days march across the wilderness, to Yellow Lake with proposals to Miss Hester Crooks. The seventh day the messenger brought me an affirmation,

and the next day I packed up my effects, swung my pack and marched."

It is significant to note how manfully the Reverend Mr. Boutwell put away the thought of having a mistress, a course of action not believed forever damning among the early pioneers, and it is also notable that Hester indulged in no untoward and maidenly delays, but gave him his answer immediately, the entire negotiations being completed in one week. The marriage ceremonies were speedily arranged and the young persons were united in "Christian and civilized form" at Fond du Lac. It is supposed that this is the first time a "Christian and civilized" marriage ceremony was ever performed in what is now Minnesota. No society reporters were present on that fall day of 1834, but there is an authenticated account of the ceremony which assures us that the affair was not without a festive note, for there was a wedding feast of tea and doughnuts, an odd combination, but one no doubt dictated by necessity.

The wedding rites duly and truly solemnized, the newlyweds began the trip to Leech Lake and arrived at the scene of Boutwell's missionary endeavor thirty-nine days after he had started for his bride. His diary reveals some interesting facts about the honeymoon trip, which was made in a canoe through dense forests, along the St. Louis River, over numerous portages to the isolated birch-bark cabin on the lake, which was soon replaced by a more pretentious structure, a log, walled cottage. His "dear Hester, like a true heart," followed him "through mud and water half-leg deep" and carried "a few kitchen utensils".

"This is a palace to me," Boutwell wrote, "though I have neither chair, stove, table or bedstead. Our windows, which are deerskins, admit a very imperfect light, scarcely sufficient to enable one to read."

In such surroundings did Hester Crooks, who was a faithful wife and the mother of seven children, start her housekeeping. Brides weren't so demanding one hundred years ago, for all that there were few eligible girls and they could afford to consider the field rather carefully before selecting a husband.

The Mankato-New Ulm imbroglio

Mankato declared war on New Ulm on the day after the Christmas of 1866. A raiding party of three hundred set out from Mankato, armed with guns and two pieces of artillery. At least all these events were reported in the papers of Minnesota. Probably they were exaggerations, but the official record certainly shows that feeling between the two towns, the county seats of Blue Earth and Brown counties, was in a mighty feverish state, and the wonder is that they didn't actually resort to arms.

The genesis of this embryonic war was in a bill for seventy-five cents worth of whiskey, or to be more accurate, in a dispute over the bill. One faction claimed that the bill should be seventy-five cents and the other insisted that this was twenty-five cents too much.

There had been a big Christmas celebration in the courthouse of New Ulm. The town had taken on a festival spirit, and among the prospective guests were George Liscomb and Alexander Campbell of Mankato, trappers. They rode into town with a friend early in the day, bringing with them about two hundred ·muskrat skins, which they sold at a store for something like twenty-five dollars. Then they set out to see what the place had to offer in the way of entertainment.

As one of the most inviting spots seemed to be the National Hall Saloon, they dropped in there for a taste of conviviality. About a dozen others were in the saloon ahead of them, all good-natured and well-behaved.

Liscomb and Campbell joined the festivities. They played cards for a time, and had one or two rounds of drinks. Before long the party became wilder. When someone suggested a dance the two visitors from Mankato pulled out their knives and hopped around the room shouting and howling in imitation of an Indian scalp dance. Someone in the saloon said that Liscomb and Campbell were half-breeds, and that didn't help their popularity in the least. It is important to remember that this was only four years after the Sioux Outbreak in 1862, when several hundred whites were butchered by the Indians. During this dance Liscomb was heard to remark that he "didn't give a damn for the Dutch," an unfortunate statement to make in New Ulm at any time. While they were doing their scalp dance, a man named John Spinner tapped the time for them by pounding on a kettle.

Time came to pay for the drinks that had been ordered by Liscomb and Campbell, and an altercation arose as to the amount. It appeared that the custom was for everyone in the saloon to step up the bar when the drinks were ordered. Anyway, the Mankato men claimed they didn't owe the seventy-five cents demanded. They said that the sum should not be more than fifty cents. Then Spinner spoke up and advised them to pay and not make trouble.

For the next few minutes all was confusion. In the melee Spinner was stabbed in the side by one of the trappers, and then both Mankato men tried to make their escape out of the back door of the saloon. Spinner, mortally wounded, nevertheless had the strength to seize a hatchet and slash Liscomb in a last desperate move for retaliation. By this time the fighting had attracted the attention of the sheriff, George Jacobs, who appeared on the scene and led the trappers off to jail. Liscomb had been so seriously hurt that he would have died from his injuries, if other events had not intervened. At the jail the sheriff ordered his captives disrobed on the pretense of searching them for weapons.

Meantime at the National Hall Saloon Spinner had died, and news of his death spread rapidly through New Ulm. On all sides it was repeated that he had been killed

by half-breed redskins. Small groups began to collect in the streets, and at about five in the afternoon, the jail was stormed by a lynching party variously estimated at from fifty to two hundred in number. The sheriff, judging from all accounts of the day, made no resistance of consequence, but permitted the crowd to take his prisoners after a small show of force. Nearly naked, the unfortunate wretches were taken outside the jail doors and promptly hanged from the iron gratings of the prison windows. Before they died they were brutally beaten. The coroner's inquest stated that "George Liscomb and Alexander Campbell died at New Ulm December 25, 1866, between three and five in the afternoon, struck with a hatchet, pounded in the head with clubs and cordwood, stabbed in the heart with knives, and hung with ropes." The New Ulm mob did a thorough job of it.

Even after the lynching was over and the crowd had slunk away, the Brown County sheriff took no action. He permitted the cold, stark bodies to lie in the yard of the courthouse. Next morning they had disappeared, but no one knew where they had been secreted. They had been seen in the yard that Christmas night as late as ten or eleven o'clock.

Next day word of the lynching was carried to Mankato and the excitement was intense. All sorts of drastic proposals were made, including one to form an army and march on New Ulm. The people of Mankato were highly incensed, for Liscomb and Campbell were not half-breeds; moreover, they were both members of Company "H", second regiment of the Minnesota militia. Their lynching was called a barbarous outrage, and Mankato was fu-

rious. The upshot was that Captain L.N. Holmes of the Mankato militia with a detachment of men went to New Ulm to investigate and, if possible, to recover the bodies of the murdered men. Clues were found that led Captain Holmes to the Minnesota River, which flows near New Ulm. On the ice were found traces of blood. A freshly cut hole, about twenty-two inches square, was discovered, and there, crammed under the ice, were the bodies of Liscomb and Campbell, mutilated more than they had been in the courthouse yard.

Not caring to risk coming into conflict with the Brown County authorities on the New Ulm side of the river, Holmes took the bodies across into Nicollet County, of which St. Peter was the county seat. While armed men stood guard over the dead and dismembered human wreckage, messengers were sent to St. Peter for a coroner, but none could be found. Under no circumstances would the bodies be delivered to the coroner of Brown County, for he was a relative of Spinner. The corpses were finally loaded on a wagon and taken to Mankato, where an inquest was conducted that revealed most of the facts concerned with the killing of Spinner and the lynching of Liscomb and Campbell. During this inquest the excitement continued to run high. It was freely said that the men had been lured to the saloon and that the intention had been to rob them. Many men known to have been in the lynching party were named at this inquest.

The whole affair was dreadful from every viewpoint, and it was years before New Ulm and Mankato were able to forget and patch up the differences created by the catastrophe of Christmas Day, 1866.

Anoka's rum rebellion!

Carrie Nation was a plagiarist after all. Her amusing little pastime of dropping unexpectedly into Kansas saloons and spilling choice vintages all over the place to the great chagrin of the bartenders was far from original. They did it at Anoka before Carrie started her meteoric career, and before she and her bar-chopping tomahawk became nearly as celebrated as young George Washington and his cherry tree hatchet.

There was a saloon war in Anoka in the spring of 1858, and when hostilities had ceased, through exhaustion on the part of the opposing forces, no doubt, there were property casualties and a hog theft, but there were no losses of life. It was a bloodless but nevertheless exciting "whiskey rebellion". The "war", which lasted about a year, began when the enterprising Daniel D. Dudley came to Anoka determined to apply his energies in commercial pursuits in that town on the Rum River. Perhaps the name of the river misled him into believing that Anoka would welcome his project of starting the "Empire Saloon" with open arms and resolutions from the commercial club, if there was a commercial club. Anyway, Daniel D. Dudley moved into a building on the main street, put in a bar and tables, rows of glistening glasses, a mirror, a brass rail, stacks and stacks of bottles – bottled "before the war" and meaning the Civil War, of course. Probably there was even a "family entrance", but of that, Albert M. Goodrich, leading historian for Anoka and Anoka County, makes no mention.

But if the grogshop-keeper had expected encouragement from the citizenry, he was promptly disappointed. Up to the time he had appeared there were no saloons in Anoka, and a considerable portion of the population was definitely convinced that there should be none there. So the aroused temperance adherents had a public meeting of indignation, with many speeches in which the evils of the "demon rum" were graphically described. Some were in favor of using peaceful means to show Dudley wherein

he erred, and a more belligerent group spoke in favor of running him out of town by force; even tar and feathers may have been suggested. However, after going over the situation in some detail, the wiser counsel prevailed and a committee of seven was delegated to call at the "Empire Saloon" and try amiably to persuade Dudley to decamp. The committee fulfilled its mission to the best of its ability, but Dudley was not impressed by their arguments. His business was good and he much resented the suggestion that he move out. When he refused point-blank, the committee reported its failure.

For another thirty days Dudley carried on his trade and prosperity came rolling in at his front door. Then one night there was a party, something like the "Boston Tea Party", for most of the intruding guests were disguised. They burst in on Dudley after closing hours, found him slumbering quietly, dreaming of next day's profits, tied him securely, and then proceeded to break up his shop and scatter his most valuable merchandise all over the street, thereby not only stealing a march on Carrie Nation but on contemporary revenue agents also.

Upon his release, indignant and stirred to action, Dudley immediately tried to find revenge through the law. He had ten or twelve suspected as participating in the raid arrested and tried for destroying his liquors. It was a remarkable trial, conducted before R.M. Johnson, a justice of the peace. Those charged by Dudley with assault were permitted to go free without bail, and so occupied were they with personal matters that many of them were simply too busy to get around to visit the courtroom when the trial was scheduled to begin. So the case was postponed again and again, and the justice took no drastic steps to get it started.

Finally, when enough of the counsel were rounded up for the trial, the culprits were faced with a recitation of their wrongdoings. One of the persons haled before the bar of justice was Benjamin Shuler. He appears to have

been spokesman for his side, and when he tired of the proceedings he initiated an amazing legal coup, never heard of before in any law court. He politely shelved the defense attorneys, arose in open court, and made a motion to the spectators that the trial be adjourned. When the perturbed justice tried to get order no one paid any attention, and Shuler put the motion. It was carried and all the accused marched out of the courtroom, never to appear again to answer to the charge. Dudley was not discouraged. He reopened his business at the same place, but tried to keep his operations more under cover. Probably his establishment was then comparable to the modern speakeasy. Everything went along well for about a year, and then one night there was a mysterious fire. When the smoke had died away his saloon was in ruins. Although no evidence was ever produced in proof, it was generally believed that the same incensed citizens who had started the raid were responsible for the fire. At any rate, such was Dudley's opinion, and his revenge was quick, pre-

sumably. A new and imposing Methodist church was being constructed, and everything was in place but the steeple. The day was about to be set for the dedication ceremonies when Anoka had another fire of unknown origin. That was the end of the Methodist church. It was considered most significant that Dudley was convinced that members of the congregation were chiefly responsible for his difficulties.

The "war" continued unabated. Dudley moved into a barn, where he sold whiskey in jugs. But he came to real grief when he stole a hog and was placed in jail. He was tried, but was set free when his attorney pointed out that he had already been imprisoned longer than the punishment for stealing would have been. Later he was convicted of forgery of a note and was shipped off to Stillwater. After his release he made a feeble attempt to begin business again, but it came to nothing, and hostilities died out without any official peace pact.

The new teacher's name of District 212 was Miss Moran. It was 1915 and if "teacher" had a first name, no one ever used it.

Each new teacher had special peculiarities. Everybody was amused because Miss Moran lugged in a gunnysack of potatoes that sat next to the water pail. She wouldn't say what they were to be used for.

Then one day the second week of December they found out.

When school started it was a bright day. By noon, clouds had obliterated the sun. Like someone was pushing a dark partition. In a few minutes it turned dark as night. The air was filled with a sifting of snow coming from all directions.

Miss Moran sent the oldest boys in her enrollment of sixteen pupils out to the coal shed with pails to carry in coal. She had them tie a twine string from the cloak room doorknob to that of the shed. They were told to dump the coal right on the floor well away from the jacket of the big old round Majestic heater. Pails of clean snow were set on top of the stove to melt for drinking.

Although it was still mid-afternoon, they had to light the lamps, burned one by one. Lunch pails were long empty and the last lamp flickered as its wick sucked it dry.

The group took turns telling stories and jokes. They sang all the songs they knew, and Miss Moran tried to read, but it was too dark. Miss Moran opened the stove door a crack for light enough for them to play tag around the seats.

It was then they began to smell the earthy odor of potatoes baking.

Miss Moran explained, "While you were playing tag, I laid the top of the stove solid with potatoes. I'd heard

about these blizzards."

After they had eaten, the desks were pushed together and the children covered with coats. Miss Moran stayed awake to watch the stove and put in more coal.

The blizzard lasted most of two days. It settled just hours

before the coal and potatoes gave out.

Everyone came through in fine spirits until they were rescued, except Miss Moran. She looked beat.

******

In 1853, the Coopers moved from New York to mid-Minnesota smack into the teeth of a blizzard. Since it was still only fall, Mr. Cooper had no warm coat. He traded two pigs to an Indian for a warm blanket. It is said that his wife made a coat from it that fit perfectly.

******

Charles Andrew Gilman, lieutenant governor of Minnesota in 1880, wrote about the winter of 1855 in Sauk Rapids.

"The mercury never got above 35 or 40 below zero. In order to keep the kids and our supply of potatoes from freezing, we put them all in one bed and covered them well. It worked. The wife and I got pretty cold, but survived."

******

Conrad Anderson had taken a load of wheat to the mill for his boss at the turn of the century.

He related, "Though it was only the first week of November, a gray blanket of tiny particles of snow like bits of ice hurled themselves at me and my team. Frost soon covered my beard. I couldn't see the horses' heads it got so dark. Ice formed over their eyes and nostrils. I got off as much of it as I could, unhitched them, and gave them a hard slap on their rumps. Then, I unloaded the wagon, turned it over, and though partially frozen, tunneled under the box and closed myself in with snow. I was soon snug and warm. It was clear and crackling cold when I crawled out the next morning...to find I was a scant half mile from home!"

******

In 1900, the Fenskes of New York Mills wrote of a blizzard that left snowdrifts around their house so deep they had to crawl out through an upstairs window.

After long hours of work, the husband and boys got the kitchen door open and the snow pressed back until

they could make a narrow tunnel to the barn where cows and calves were bellowing.

One storm after another piled more snow on top. They used the tunnel for the next several months and it proved to be a fine way to get to the barn without feeling the biting wind.

One day the neighbor's bull wandered over the hard crust that had formed on top. He fell through, landing on his back with all four feel flailing the air, bellowing for all he was worth. Churning the snow caused more to collapse over him. Finally, after putting in the hardest work of a winter filled with hard labor, the Fenske's got him shoveled out an exit and he high-tailed it for home, never to return.

******

Countless stories, morbid but true, can be found telling of people found frozen in grotesque shapes. In many cases they could have saved themselves by using common sense.

It has been proven that snow makes a fine insulation against the cold if done right. Care must be taken to leave a small vent for steam to escape. Many saved themselves from freezing only to be smothered as heat from the body forms a glaze over the small cavity they have dug for themselves, which is airtight.

In either case...they are quite as dead.

While stories of deaths from blizzards abound, it was seldom that a dumb (?) animal, if left to roam free, was ever found. Some innate sense of preservation seemed to tell them the right thing to do. Often, if given their heads, a team took their master directly to his own barn.

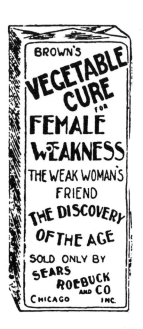

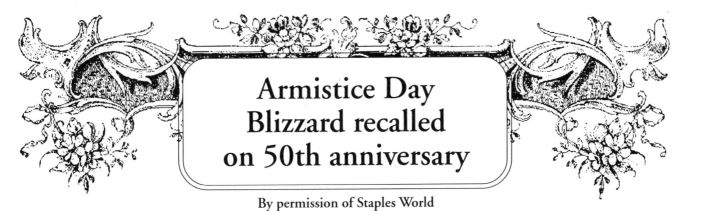

Armistice Day Blizzard recalled on 50th anniversary

By permission of Staples World

Those who survived it, remember it.

Termed the blizzard of the century and recalled for its suddenness, local residents this week recalled, some of the events surrounding the famous Armistice Day blizzard of November 11, 1940.

Pat Young of Staples remembered being caught out in the field picking corn. "We were picking corn by hand that day. Boy, did that snow ever come down!"

Drifts piled up in the roads and in the fields, Young said, causing problems for picking corn for the rest of the winter. His family was normally still picking corn in November, but no one expected a story of such severity that early.

"We got most of it picked over that winter, but it was a lot harder. Winter just came a little early that year," Young, who farmed east of Staples, said.

Like most of those who remember the Armistice Day blizzard, Young is now retired but still lives east of town.

Jim Hammond of Staples remembers getting called in to work at the Northern Pacific depot. "There must have been 12-foot drifts on the Sixth Street crossing," Hammond said. His boss had to come and get him. "We couldn't see your hand in front of your face."

Hammond told how crews of men and horses were used to move snow from the platform south of the depot. "We moved snow from the depot platform on the south side over to the east, near Dr. Lund's office. By the time we got back for another load, you couldn't tell we had been there."

But it wasn't too much longer before all the passenger and freight trains were cancelled. Then the snow was just allowed to pile up.

The storm took over 30 lives in Minnesota. It rolled in on Sunday, November 11, and continued through Tuesday, paralyzing both local and statewide activity. According to that week's Staples World, there was light precipitation Saturday evening. Sunday the snow continued falling, but not until Sunday night did it develop into blizzard proportions.

The 16-inch snowfall recorded by the Twin Cities was the largest amount ever recorded in one winter storm.

In the Staples area a number of farm losses were recorded, including some 2,400 turkeys lost by a farmer near Sebeka. Another flock of about 1,200 were lost near Perham. Both were to be marketed through the Severson Produce Company of Staples. Other turkey flocks in the area also suffered heavy losses. A few lucky farmers had already sent most of their birds to market.

Bernita Jasmer, now of Aldrich, was a senior at the time at Hewitt High School. Her father had brought her into town so she could take part in class play rehearsals, and she planned to stay the weekend at an uncle's house." "I walked across the street to the school and the wind just about blew me away. I couldn't even see across the street."

Things were not flush on the farm in those days, she recalled. Her father had been feeding out a herd of hogs, and they were just ready for market. "Just before the storm, I remember the truck coming to the farm and picking up the hogs to take them to South St. Paul. I remember Dad sitting in the house after they were gone, figuring out how much he would make on those hogs.

"But we never got paid. That truck got stalled on the other side of Clarissa and every animal on it froze to death. It made for a long winter," she said.

Kenny Cleveland of Staples also recalled the big snow drifts on Sixth Street. "The snow was so deep, they couldn't

get the doors on the old fire hall opened," he said.

According to the Staples World, that Monday night a fire destroyed the Spillane and Button buildings in Aldrich. The Spillane building housed the Spillane Tavern and the Cut Rate Store, while the other building housed a soft drink parlor and lunch room operated by Al Resseguire. The World said the Staples Fire Department could not get out of the city.

The storm disrupted personal plans for a holiday weekend for many, with the pages of the World containing numerous examples of people forced to make extended visits or unable to get back for work.

Two young teachers from the Staples area had very similar experiences. Hazel Vasecka, who was Hazel Buckingham in 1940, taught at District 25 school on the Nimrod road, but had gone to her parents near Hubbard for the weekend. "I didn't get back to school until that next Thursday. Boy, was I worried" she said this week.

Kathryn (Tils) Berg, who has lived all her life just northwest of Staples, was supposed to be at the District 20 school north of Aldrich for classes. "My dad and a neighbor tried to get me from our farm to the school. I was driving and they were shoveling. After they shoveled, I would drive ahead, get stuck, and they shoveled some more. We made about three miles and then turned around and went

home."

The pages of the World told how Della Carry, teacher at District 91 in the Moran-Germania area, didn't get back until Wednesday evening from her parents home near Cushing. Then she had to walk over five miles until Roland Thiel was able to meet her with a team. The snow banks were so deep that the horses just could not get through. School was held Thursday and Friday, however.

It was a busy week for garages and tow trucks as hundreds of Armistice Day travelers, duck hunters and others were marooned in snow drifts. Some 35 cars and buses were stuck in the drifts near Long Prairie. About 100 people were stuck in a small tavern at Becker for two days. Margaret Anderson of Staples recalled a girl friend who had to spend the storm on a pool table at a tavern in Perham. "The girls slept on the table, the guys on the floor." she said.

Other storms since then have eclipsed the Armistice Day blizzard, with it now ranking as the fourth worst storm on record. The worst was January 10-12, 1975, when 100 m.p.h. winds rocked the state for two days and sent the barometer to 28.4 inches, the lowest reading ever in the state.

But that doesn't stop those who remember the Armistice Day storm from noting with pride that they survived that big blizzard.

The Carlisle train robbery

Everything appeared to be all set for a quiet fall in Otter Tail County in 1898. Some of the boys were beginning to trickle back from Cuba, the Philippines, and other places after having given the Spaniards a sound beating; harvesting was all over and there was little plowing left to be done. Nothing seemed likely to turn up that would create any excitement around Fergus Falls and neighboring towns.

But just as everyone was getting resigned to a tranquil winter, up turned a series of incidents that gave the entire district something to talk about for months on end. Incidentally, in surveying these incidents from a distance of something like thirty-three years, one sees considerable humor in them, but no one could see anything funny in the situation at the time.

It now appears that five men were sent off to Stillwater for a crime they didn't commit, but since they were bad ones and perhaps even deserved to be hung, there was no sympathy wasted on them in 1898.

The Oriental Limited, a crack train of the Great Northern, had swung out of Fergus Falls in a cloud of smoke and steam early in the evening of November 10. It had left the Twin Cities a few hours before, north bound with a heavy consignment of passengers.

There were four or five passengers on board, however, who were traveling contraband. When the train paused for a few seconds at Fergus Falls, they had secreted themselves on the blind baggage without going through the formality of telling any of the train crew that they wished transportation.

A few miles up the line the rails crossed the Pelican River. Here two of these non-paying guests climbed over the tender and politely but firmly covered the engineer with guns and instructed him to proceed a short distance and then stop the train. Meanwhile, other bandits had scattered over the train, and when the engineer discreetly

obeyed orders, the robbers had everything well in hand and there was nothing to be done to interfere with their plans. No passenger was permitted to leave the coaches to give an alarm. Even the headlight on the engine was extinguished for fear of attracting the attention of some observant farmer. The train had stopped near the present site of Carlisle.

The engineer and the fireman were ordered to leave the cab and sit quietly on the bank, guarded by a robber, while the baggage and expressmen were told to open the door of their car, a command they refused to obey. A blast of dynamite quickly made an impromptu entrance to the baggage car, through which armed men rushed to capture the inmates, who were made to join the engineer and the fireman on the bank. The conductor and the brakeman tried to come to the rescue of their brother trainmen, but a sharp gun fire drove them back.

For the next hour the robbers tried desperately to force open the safe in the baggage car without success. They then considered going through the pockets of all the passengers, but they feared that some of them were armed and gave up that scheme. Thwarted on every side, they were obliged to make off in the darkness, their entire loot being the twenty dollars they had forced the engineer to surrender. As soon as they were out of the way the train went on to Barnesville, where news was flashed of the train holdup. Posses were organized to scour the country, telegrams were sent out in all directions, and other determined steps were taken to apprehend the miscreants.

The excitement was especially great because there had been numerous bank robberies and minor burglaries committed in the vicinity about this time. It was believed the train robbers were a part of a desperate gang that was terrorizing the country. In 1898 Breckenridge and Moorhead were headquarters for all sorts of rough characters. Both towns were wet, and right across the state line was North

Dakota, a dry state.

At about daybreak on the morning following the Oriental Limited stickup, four men entered the Exchange Hotel, near the Northern Pacific station in Moorhead, and went to bed. A little later they were joined by two other men, all suspicious looking individuals. The clerk telephoned Murphy, chief of police at Moorhead, who arrested the entire outfit and took them off to jail, a quick enough capture to satisfy anyone, provided the prisoners had been the train robbers. In the possession of the men were discovered tools used by burglars, dynamite and various other articles indicating that they were the guilty persons.

The prisoners were taken in handcuffs back to Fergus Falls, where they were met on the platform of the Northern Pacific station by fifteen hundred curious persons. On the march up to the jail one of the captives put his handcuffed hands in his pocket and, so posing as one of the spectators, almost made his escape.

Naturally the affair made a great stir in Otter Tail County and throughout the state. Detectives from Minneapolis went to Fergus Falls to try to identify the men. They were photographed despite their objections, and it was soon established that all had criminal records.

The December term of court came and the men were put on trial on charges of robbing the train and a bank at Warfield. They were indicted under the names of Link Thayer, Charles Hoffman, Homer D. Minot, James E. Edwards, Wallace C. Ross, and James C. Hall. The indicted men insisted they were innocent and demanded that they be tried at once, a wish that was speedily gratified. It was almost a foregone conclusion that they would be found guilty. The community was in no mood for trifling. Crimes had been done and there must be punishment. Besides, didn't these men have criminal records? And what about the incriminating evidence that had been found on their persons?

The trials were so interesting that the courthouse was crowded every day while the cases were being heard. C.L. Hilton, later to become attorney general of Minnesota, was one of the lawyers. The cases dragged along all winter and gave everyone plenty to talk about. The train robbery and speculation about the fate of the culprits relieved the tedium of long winter nights.

Along in the spring of 1899 the trials were concluded; all the accused men with the exception of Ross were sent to Stillwater.

They had been guests of the state for only a short time, however, when strenuous efforts were made to prove that they were not the guilty men and that they had had no connection whatever with the Carlisle train holdup. It was contended that the six men were in the vicinity to promote a series of burglaries and that they were preparing to do a job at Larimore when they were captured by the Moorhead chief of police. Naturally, at their trials, they had been greatly embarrassed. They had been guilty of so many misdeeds that an admission of them probably would have brought as severe penalties as to permit themselves to be tried for a train affair.

It came to be believed by those in a position to know that a band of robbers had come to Minnesota from Missouri, and that they had made arrangements with a bribable official at Breckenridge for protection. The plan was for them to hold up the train at Carlisle, make away with their booty and be met by this official and taken to safety. Something is supposed to have gone wrong with their plans. They didn't meet the official but spent the night in a haystack; the next day they fled south and out of the state. They are thought to have reached Missouri, where they did time for some other crime.

Even at the time so much question was raised as to the guilt of the men who had been sent to Stillwater that they were released after serving but a small part of their terms. It was generally believed that their incarceration couldn't have done them any harm, whether they were guilty of the train robbery or not.

In spite of their release the Great Northern paid the reward it had offered for the capture of the men who had held up the Oriental Limited and, take it all around, no one, not even the men who had served short terms, complained much about the outcome of the whole matter. If all the facts about them had been known, they might still be there today.

The South Haven bandit raid!

There were strenuous days in the state and nation back in 1903. That was the year Admiral Schley, one of the heroes of the Spanish-American War, recommended a certain patent medicine as a sure cure for catarrh; James J. Jeffries gave James J. Corbett a sound trouncing; and Minnesota was stirred by a bandit raid and battle near South Haven, in Wright County. This battle never brought South Haven as much prominence as the James and Younger boys gave Northfield, but it was quite a fracas, and before it was over plenty of ammunition was used, and there were dead and wounded, and the "tramps" were safely housed in the Hennepin County jail. They called them "tramps" in those days. No one thought of dignifying desperadoes by referring to them as "gangsters" or "gunmen".

One of the remarkable things about this battle was that the two men who were instrumental in effecting the capture of the bandits went through a shower of bullets, only to die later in a more unusual manner. One of these men was W.G. Young, the sheriff. He came out of the affray with nothing more serious than a hole in his hat. The other was his deputy, John Nugent, Jr. The father of Nugent is still referred to as the most popular man who ever lived in Wright County. He was a Democrat in a strong Republican county, but he was elected sheriff for term after term, when all other members of his ticket were swamped by their opponents' ballots. For twenty-five years he was sheriff, and besides that, was United States marshal for Minnesota, postmaster of Buffalo, and president of the Sheriffs' Association of the state. His son won so much fame for himself in the South Haven battle that Wright County later elected him sheriff, too.

The late summer and fall of 1903 were seasons of lawlessness in Minnesota. Roving gangs of determined ruffians terrorized many communities in the state, robbing stores and farm houses and engaging in a campaign of holdups and general thievery. One of these gangs was operating in Wright County, helping itself generously to whatever it fancied. One day early in October the five men in the outfit walked into the store of H.T. Gunnary of Annandale, made away with one hundred dollars in cash and about a hundred dollars worth of goods, and started off in the general direction of South Haven.

Sheriff Young and Nugent took the first train in from Buffalo for South Haven, prepared to arrest the men. As they left the train at their destination, someone told them that one of the thieves was boarding the same train. He was taken into custody and delivered to the constable of South Haven, who lodged him in a grain elevator nearby. Next the officers learned that other members of the bandit crew had established themselves in an empty freight car, where they had blandly opened a store, offering for sale the merchandise they had stolen in Annandale. Young and Nugent climbed into the car and called on the men to surrender. One spoke up and said they would go along as soon as they had their dinner, and, when the sheriff curtly told them they would be fed at the hotel, the excitement began.

Young whipped out his pistol and covered one of the men while Nugent was searching another in the far end of the car. Quietly a bandit crept up behind the deputy and banged him over the head. The sound attracted Young, and for a moment he permitted his eyes to glance away from the man he was covering. When he turned back, he found four guns pointed directly at him. When ordered to throw up his hands, he discreetly accepted the advice.

Both officers were then disarmed and marched along the railroad track to the elevator, where the first bandit was being held. Using the sheriff and his deputy as shields, they freed him. Then the bandits lined their captives up against the building with bullets for artistic materials. When they had enjoyed themselves thoroughly in this manner, to the chagrin of the unfortunate guardians of the law, they abandoned the fun and set off for safety in the surrounding woods and fields.

The town was aroused and a quick checkup revealed that there wasn't a single rifle in the place and there were only a few shotguns and revolvers – not much artillery to use in the pursuit of desperate gun-toters. The chase was taken up nevertheless, with the two officers, smarting under their humiliation, heading the posse.

One party commandeered a handcar and sped down the Soo Railroad tracks in the direction the bandits had taken. Others joined the chase on horseback and in buggies. When the pursued robbers were definitely located in a small wood, the sheriff divided his forces into three groups, and the assault was begun. A plan of campaign was laid out, but the bandits heard every word of the conversation and stole away to another wood. However, guards had been placed at the strategic points, and their new hiding place was soon made known to the posse. When the miscreants saw that they were discovered, they made ready for battle, and the fighting began.

For some time the struggle continued furiously. One of the besieged men was killed and, shortly afterward, the others asked for terms, which were announced as "unconditional surrender". The bandits gave themselves up, most of them suffering from wounds. The posse had no casualties to report, although there were some narrow escapes.

Because the jail at Buffalo was not large enough to accommodate the captives, they were taken to Minneapolis and confined in the Hennepin County lockup, greatly to the disgust of some of the taxpayers of Wright County, who objected to the prices charged by Hennepin County for incarcerating out-of-town prisoners.

At the December, 1903, term of court the four surviving members of the gang were brought back to Buffalo to be tried on various charges. There were some attempts at jail-breaking, none of them successful. The men pleaded guilty and were given terms in the penitentiary at Stillwater.

In the freight car at South Haven, where the men had started their store-keeping, were found large quantities of dynamite and other materials for systematic looting.

Young never ran for sheriff again. He was heard to say that he had had enough after the South Haven episode. He moved to Canby, Minnesota, and when fires broke out there in 1918, he joined the fighters. He was trapped in an old well, where he had jumped to escape the flames, and perished.

Nugent, who, like Young, had come through the hail of bandit bullets unharmed, was later elected sheriff. One night he went to a creamery near Buffalo to capture a man stealing butter. The creamery man was Richard Crawford. The two men arranged to take turns watching for the thief, but in some way they got their signals confused and Crawford killed Nugent.

Not a graveyard!

Fred Linnell stuck callused hands deep into pockets of overalls eligible for the rag-bag long ago. He kicked a scoop of sand toward an anemic row of corn eight inches high. It was already the middle of July. It looked more yellow than green, too.

People teased Fred that he had more hair in his eyebrows than he had on his head. He couldn't deny it. His eyebrows were the bristly kind that stuck straight out about an inch. Below them darted a pair of alert bright blue eyes that missed nothing. Those eyebrows always made him look crabby, when actually he wasn't.

On the other hand, if he was so "alert", how'd he ever let himself be talked into this mess? He'd hate to think his love for fishing, and this was near Long Lake west of Osage, that did it.

The mess he had gotten into was selling a halfway productive farm at Sebeka for a patch of yellow sand that had sent the Lord only knows how many families to the poorhouse over the years. Any water needed had to come from a well at Long Lake, a mile or more away. He wondered, was there water enough in the big can to even make coffee this morning?

Grandpa's cooking was avoided by anyone not equipped with galvanized innards. It was said a spoon could stand straight up in a cup of his coffee. Everything he cooked was covered with a layer of black pepper so thick it hid whatever was under it.

Grandpa Fred ambled toward an oversized log cabin. It was both wider and longer by far than most. He stopped and looked around. When Sarah moved up from the place at Sebeka, it would look different. Women always did things with curtains, rugs, plants at the window. She'd sure think she had to grow things. But in this sand?

They had to have a well, that's what! She could water a small garden. That'd make her feel better. She didn't like making this move anyhow, and he didn't blame her. Liked

to have kicked himself!

Fred knew that all he had to do was mention the need to the boys and they'd take care of it. They were pretty good boys...if you didn't take your eyes off 'em. He grinned, remembering that he had been somewhat of a hellion himself when he was their age.

A few weeks later Hugh and Rus arrived with the tools they needed, some pipe and a pump. Wives came with hot dishes and cake. It would be easy to drive a sandpoint. Fred headed for Osage for something the women needed and the boys went out to start the well.

"You know, Rus, if we dug down eight or ten feet, Ma'd have a place to keep things cool. She could let milk, butter and set jello in fruit jars and let them down on a twine string. After that, we could drive the point down from there. Right?"

Rus considered. "Yeah, we'd have to shore up the sides with boards in this sand."

Within minutes the sand was flying with both of them shirtless as they dug. Finally they fitted in four boards to make a frame, then dug down again. They took turns getting into the well after it got down a ways. The sand was easy to shovel and by the middle of the afternoon they were down about eight feet.

"That's deep enough, Hughie. Give me a hand and I'll boost you out," Rus said.

Before he could agree, Hugh felt the first sprinkles of sand on his back. Then a board took him on the shoulder and an avalanche of sand headed his way.

Ducking his head and squinting his eyes shut, he started to run. It seemed he was getting no where, then he'd hear Rus yelling, "C'mon, boy! You can do it! Faster, faster, another foot or so and I can reach you. Keep a comin'! Hold up your hand!"

Rus wrestled at many fairs and when he grabbed Hugh's hand and gave a yank, Hugh saw daylight and got his first

breath of clear air. Drenched with sweat and covered with sand, he looked like something from another planet as he collapsed on a pile of sand.

"Didn't know I could run five miles in one spot," he gasped.

Then from sheer thankfulness and being together, they howled with laughter, slapping each other on the back. The hole had filled in again with sand, almost to the top. The women came out of the cabin, not thinking it was so funny.

About that time the old Ford rattled into the yard, coming to a stop near them. Getting out, their dad saw at a glance what had happened...and that he had almost lost his youngest son! There was sudden silence, with only the wind in the big pines behind the cabin to break it.

"You durned, #@&*^)! crazy young fools! I asked for a WELL! Not a GRAVEYARD! Now get the sand outta your eyes and drive that point down like I said. Shouldn't take long...but you're going to get it done tonight if I have to light the lantern! Ma needs water!"

Sobered by the experience, and realizing that their dad was right, they went back to work. Not long before it was time to light the lantern the first gushes of yellowish water came from the spout of the pump.

I can still remember them laughing around the supper table about the time Uncle Hughie ran at least five miles in one spot.

PLEASE COMPLETE THE FOLLOWING TO ORDER ADDITIONAL COPIES

Please send me _____ additional books at **$24.95 each** *(plus $3.50 shipping & handling)*

SEND THIS ORDER FORM TO:
McCleery & Sons Publishing
PO Box 248
Gwinner, ND 58040-0248

I am enclosing $_____
❑ Check ❑ Money Order

Payable in US funds. No cash accepted.

SHIP TO:
Name_____
Mailing Address _____
City _____
State/Zip _____

For credit card orders call 1-888-568-6329

Bill my: ❑ VISA ❑ MasterCard   Expires _____
Card # _____
Signature _____
Daytime Phone Number _____

OR Order On-Line at
www.jmcompanies.com

Shipping and Handling costs for larger quantites available upon request.

Orders by check allow longer delivery time.

Money order and credit card orders will be shipped within 48 hours.

This offer is subject to change without notice.

Charlie's Gold
and Other Frontier Tales
Kamron's first collection of short stories gives you adventure tales about men and women of the west, made up of cowboys, Indians, and settlers. Written by Kent Kamron.
(174 pgs.)
$15.95 each in a 6x9" paperback.
(plus $3.50 ea.shipping & handling)

A Time For Justice
This second collection of Kamron's short stories takes off where the first volume left off, satisfying the reader's hunger for more tales of the wide prairie.
Written by Kent Kamron.
(182 pgs.)
$16.95 each in a 6x9" paperback.
(plus $3.50 ea. shipping & handling)

Bonanza Belle
In 1908, Carrie Amundson left her home to become employed on a bonanza farm. One tragedy after the other befell her and altered her life considerably and she found herself back on the farm.
Written by Elaine Ulness Swenson.
(344 pgs.)
$15.95 each in a 6x8-1/4" paperback.
(plus $3.50 ea. shipping & handling)

First The Dream
This story spans ninety years of Anna's life. She finds love, loses it, and finds in once again. A secret that Anna has kept is fully revealed at the end of her life.
Written by Elaine Ulness Swenson.
(326 pgs.)
$15.95 each in a 6x8-1/4" paperback.
(plus $3.50 ea. shipping & handling)

Country-fied
Stories with a sense of humor and love for country and small town people who, like the author, grew up country-fied . . . Country-fied people grow up with a unique awareness of their dependence on the land. They live their lives with dignity, hard work, determination and the ability to laugh at themselves.
Written by Elaine Babcock.
(184 pgs.)
$14.95 each in a 6x9" paperback.
(plus $3.50 ea. shipping & handling)

Dr. Val Farmer's
Honey, I Shrunk The Farm
The first volume in a three part series of Rural Stress Survival Guides discusses the following in seven chapters: Farm Economics; Understanding The Farm Crisis; How To Cope With Hard Times; Families Going Through It Together; Dealing With Debt; Going For Help, Helping Others and Transitions Out of Farming.
Written by Val Farmer. (208 pgs.)
$16.95 each in a 6x9" paperback.
(plus $3.50 ea. shipping & handling)

Pay Dirt
An absorbing story reveals how a man with the courage to follow his dream found both gold and unexpected adventure and adversity in Interior Alaska, while learning that human nature can be the most unpredictable of all.
Written by Otis Hahn &
Alice Vollmar. (168 pgs.)
$15.95 each in a 6x9" paperback.
(plus $3.50 ea. shipping & handling)

Pete's New Family
Pete's New Family is a tale for children (ages 4-8) lovingly written to help youngsters understand events of divorce that they are powerless to change.
Written by Brenda Jacobson.
$9.95 each in a 5-1/2x8-1/2" spiral bound book.
(plus $2.50 ea. shipping & handling)
(price breaks after qty. of 10)

Prayers For Parker Cookbook
Parker Sebens is a 3 year old boy from Milnor, ND, who lost both of his arms in a tragic farm accident on September 18, 2000. He has undergone many surgeries to reattach his arms, but because his arms were damaged so extensively and the infection so fierce, they were unable to save his hands. Parker will face many more surgeries in his future, plus be fitted for protheses.

This cookbook is a project of the Country Friends Homemakers Club from Parker's community. All profits from the sale of this book will go to the Parker Sebens' Benefit Fund, a fund set up to help with medical-related expenses due to Parker's accident.
$8.00 ea. in a 5-1/4"x8-1'4" spiral bound book.
(plus $2.00 ea. shipping & handling)